A HISTORY OF ANGELS CAMP

Printed in the United States of America by Sheridan Books, Inc., Chelsea, MI 48118
First Printing, March 2001
Second Printing, March 2004
Third Printing, November 2006
Fourth Printing, August 2012

Library of Congress Catalog Card Number: 2001086253

ISBN 0-9749527-0-2

e-mail address: purdyboy@goldrush.com

Published by Haddon House Press
P.O. Box 592, Altaville, CA 95221
Telephone: (209) 736-6886

A History of
Angels Camp

Plus: A Walking Tour

by

H. Stuart Manners

Photograph Acknowledgement

Most of the photographs and visual art in this book are the property of the Calaveras County Historical Society. We gratefully thank the society for the use of these photos.

A few of the photographs and visual art are the property of other entities. They can be identified by the "credit" shown under each photo or map. We thank them for their courtesy and generosity for allowing us to include them in this volume.

Informational Acknowledgement

The author gratefully acknowledges the encouragement and assistance by literally dozens of people interested in telling the story of Angels Camp: Fenton Bolton, Dufo Gualdoni, Loren Whittle, Rich Cathcart, Vicki and Duane Oneto, Roy Sorocco, George Baratono, Alan Corell, Cleve Haynes, Walter Valente, Jack Dillashaw, Nelda Quinones, Faye and Don Fletcher, Mattie Vierra, Lolly Ver Halen, Dodie Freed, Barbara Richards, Pearl and Dave Cosgrave, Paul Raggio, Mike Fullaway, Pat BullFin, Andrea Brown, Sharon Fleming, Ruby Minard, and many others. A special thanks for assistance "beyond the call of duty" to Elizabeth Braydis, Office Manager, and Cate Culver, both on staff of Calaveras County Historical Society, and to Lorrayne Kennedy, Archivest for the Calaveras County Archives.

Preface

   I've been wanting to get started on this project for several years, but "other things" kept me from it. People that I confided with continually said, "You'd better get going, 'cause all of the oldtimers are dying off." Now I wish I had started earlier. Several of the important oldtimers have become infirmed to the point that I have not been able to interview them adequately. But, many are still alive and active. I was able to talk with most of them, but not all. Yes, you may find some holes in some subjects, but I think most have turned out to be relatively complete. It has taken eleven months for the project. I welcome constructive criticism, even encourage it.

   At first, I was worried that there wouldn't be enough information available to write a book on Angels Camp. Boy, was I wrong. We Calaveras citizens are very, very fortunate to have such an excellent and active Historical Society. The archives at the society's headquarters is jam-packed with information, photos and peripheral data. It is well catalogued, with a competent and courteous staff. The county also has a valuable source of historical information at the *Archives*. It, too, has an excellent and helpful staff. About three months into writing this history, I had to decide how much information _not_ to include in the book, i.e., if an interesting story about something took place, let's say, in Murphys, but had a minor relationship with an Angels Camp story, it had to be left out, in the interest of both economics and keeping the thrust in Angels Camp.

   I'd like to plug the continuing need of the Historical Society's archives to grow and expand. If you have any pictures, photos or written artifacts, it is extremely important that you donate them to the society. They will be preserved with lots of t.l.c. Give them a call. ....and I hope you enjoy reading this book.

H. Stuart Manners

Table of Contents

COVER PHOTO: A very early photo of Downtown Main Street, Angels Camp, circa 1880. (Graphic artist, Sandi Young)

FRONTISPIECE PHOTO: The city at the peak of mining, an easterly view, with Utica's "cross shaft" hoisting works atop the hill. In the foreground is the "Chicken Ladder" sidewalk along steep Hardscrable Lane.

Chapter One

THE EARLY DAYS

It was a warm summer afternoon when members of the Carson party were out prospecting in the rolling hills of what was to become Calaveras County. They came upon a roaring creek. Plenty of water, they thought. Time to try for some "color". In no time at all, Henry P. Angel, a member of the party, and native of Rhode Island, decided to set down and locate his trading post there. There were a few prospectors in the area, but by the end of that year there were many hundreds of men working the streams and surfaces. It was July, 1848, Marshall had just "discovered" gold six months before at Coloma, and America was looking westward. American sovereignty of the California Territory had just been established by treaty with Mexico, but the territory was two years away from statehood. Here, in Angels Trading Post, was the beginning of one of the most famous and rich gold mining efforts in the entire foothill territory.

James H. Carson, a native Virginian, was the leader of the mining expedition that set out from Texas by way of Monterey,

California. Just under 100 men were in the party. Among those in the group were Henry and George Angel, Dr. I. C. Isabel, Daniel and John Murphy, William K. Casement and Edward Murphy. Most of the men in the Carson party were veterans of the Mexican War which had just concluded. The timing was ideal for these men to venture into a new life. Henry Angel settled in on the creek that would bear his name. The Murphy brothers continued on eastward a few miles, and James Carson settled on a creek and hill that would later bear his name. Carson Hill turned out to be one of the richest gold mines anywhere in the world, and was mined actively for a century and a half, until it was finally closed in 1990.

While Henry Angel was really an adventurer and a gambler, he was set to not only try his hand at mining gold but to open a trading post. In no time he was the prime supplier of over 300 local prospectors. He also became a major trader with other mining camps such as Vallecito, Murphys, Carson Hill and Douglas Flat. The population of Angel's Trading Post grew to nearly 4,000 in just a few years, and the town came to be known as Angels Camp. All of the gold mining during this early time was surface mining. Placer deposits were said to be incredibly rich, with one claim ten feet square yielding $9,000. Arrastras were used to crush any rock that needed crushing. The "Long Tom" and the "Rocker" were also used extensively, all three of which were crude methods for extracting gold from the earth.

In 1849 the Angel's Trading Post was taken over by John Scribner and Captain Henry Mathews. They built a stone building after the fire of 1855 and moved the trading post. Their location later came to be known as the Wells Fargo Building.

Another fire occurred the following year, which claimed the home of John Scribner and the life of Captain Mathews. In the meantime, John Peirano's store was opened on the south bank of Angels Creek. He, too, later built a stone building on Main Street and Birds Way, which became the "main corner" of downtown.

The original eastbound road out of the downtown area ran down Birds Way, crossed the creek, and continued up the hill. It wasn't until the State installed the "new" Angels Creek present-day bridge that the eastward turnoff was moved south a half block, and Birds Way became a blind street.

Pierano Store, southeast corner of Main Street and Birds Way

Michael Cosgrove built his livery stable on Main Street, not far from Angels Creek. Alexander Love built his stable further up Main Street, where he also built his home which faced on Bush Street. Bennager and Maria Rasberry were next-door neighbors.

An early-day history published in 1892 by the Lewis Printing Company, tells about the goings on in Calaveras and the five counties to our south. It said, "There is hardly a place today existing in California about which hangs more of the glamour and romance of the early mining days than Angel's, or, as it was formerly universally known, 'Angel's Camp,' after its pioneer.

"As early as 1849 it became one of the principal camps of the gold region, and its importance increased for several years thereafter. "It was the abiding place of Smiley, who inflicted upon Mark Twain the story of the "Jumping Frog" of Abner Dean, and through him upon the world; of the great humorist himself, and of Bret Harte; of James Gillis, Mark Twain's early partner; of

"Charcoal Jim" who remained after all the rest were gone, a relic of the olden days."

Going back about 50 years before Henry Angel and James Carson first saw this part of the territory, a man by the name of Gabriel Moraga led an exploratory party through the area. He was a Spanish Army lieutenant, and thought to be the first known non-native white man to enter the Calaveras territory. As a matter of fact, it was he who gave the area its name of Calaveras, and it was ironic that he was serving a country (Spain) that had always been on the lookout for gold in their New World territories. He missed this one. The year was 1806, and Moraga found skulls laying along the banks of a river that he named the Calaveras (Spanish for "Skulls") River.

Twenty-two years later another Spanish expedition came through the area in order to put down a rebellion by an Indian leader by the name of Estanislao, whose camp was on the river below Melones. John C. Fremont anglicized the name on a later expedition, and named the river Stanislaus in honor of this famous native. It is thought that probably others, notably Jed Smith and John Bidwell had come through the area, but did not stop for any length of time.

Transportation in Angels Camp consisted of stage lines and freight teams. It was 23 miles from Angels to Milton, and another 71 from Milton to Sacramento. The roads were the crudest, and railroads were a half-century away. It was very difficult to travel or transport freight. Horses were almighty and livery stables flourished along with blacksmith shops. The Antelope Trail was one of the first routes from Stockton, through Jenny Lind and up to Altaville and beyond. Another trail from Stockton went through Valley Springs, Double Springs and on to San Andreas and beyond.

The 1850 population of the entire state of California was 91,635. That same year the population of Calaveras County was

16,884. That is over 18% of the state's population. Just under 99% of those in the county were male (16,500), and of those 22% were of Chinese decent (3,657). The overall population of the county rose a little in the next year or two, but by 1860 it was back to the 1850 level. The surface gold was disappearing, and gold and silver strikes were popping up elsewhere, causing a major decline in local populations. By 1890 the county could boast only 8,895 citizens. Then, things picked up. The mines started producing richer ores, and consolidation of claims and mines created a more attractive environment. By the year 1900 the county population reached 11,200 residents. Another decline took place in each ensuing decade, and the county-wide population did not reach the (year) 1900 level until 1970. Banking, as we know it, was also a half-century away. The first newspaper, *The Mountaineer* published by R. V. Chadd, didn't appear until February 1872. There were bars everywhere, as needed. Schools were casual during the first days. The first school was opened in 1854, and located in a rented room owned by Bennager Rasberry at the corner of Main Street and Rasberry Lane. The teacher was John Brickell. The Protestants were the first to establish a church (1859).

The first "real" hotel in Angels Camp was the Angels Hotel, built in 1851 by C. C. Lake. It was a canvas structure, located on the northeast corner of Main Street at Birds Way, or Chinatown Road. The canvas was replaced within the first year with a one-story wooden building. In 1855, Mr. Lake decided to replace the wooden structure with a one-story stone structure. He held his "Grand Ball" opening on January 1, 1856. The stone building survived, and was so successful that he added a second story the following year. His builder, and stone mason, was Allen Taylor who subsequently built other stone structures in Angels Camp. C. C. Lake sold his hotel in 1863 to George C. Tryon, who came to Angels Camp in '49, was a very well-respected citizen, successful miner, and one-term sheriff of the county. He managed the hotel for twenty-four years, then sold to Otto and Mary Stickle Dolling in 1887. The Dollings expanded the operation by building

Angels Hotel, built in 1855-56, a landmark "par excellence"

an addition next door, and constructing a Hall on Circus Hill in the area behind the hotel. They took great pride in developing an envious reputation for fine cuisine and service. Their ownership ended with John and Ralph Lemue's purchase of the property in 1927. The Lemues continued the tradition and reputation. Today's hotel, purchased in 1962 by Gerald W. Heintz, is a transformation into an attractive apartment complex. The hotel still stands today, with recognition from the State of California Department of Parks and Recreation as California Historical Landmark No. 734. This is the actual location where Mark Twain heard the yarn that would drive him to write *The Celebrated Jumping Frog of Calaveras County.*

A blacksmith shop in Altaville was operated by Andy Gardiner and J. M. Wooster in 1854. In no time the demand for machinery in the mines led C. B. Demarest and G. D. Orcutts to establish The Altaville Foundry. This foundry and another in Sutter Creek came to be the only two in the Mother Lode. Both are continuing to operate today, but under very different modes. Altaville Foundry has changed its name to California Electric Steel Company, has moved to new digs four blocks away, has modernized to accommodate today's requirements, and has continued its daily foundry operation even during its move in 1986. It boasts, "the oldest continuous foundry operation west of the Mississippi". On the other hand, Sutter Creek's Knight Foundry, established in 1873, has continued to operate with original methods, original equipment, and powered by its original source of power, *WATER*. A recent change of ownership by a non-profit foundation has assured its operation well into the future.

Other early businesses were a bakery, drug store, butcher shop, medical offices, a carriage factory, lawyers, lumber yard, undertakers and other merchants. The first post office came to Angels Camp in 1853, and the first babies born were Andrew Crooks and Charles Cosgrove.

Water is always a problem when cities and towns grow. The water in Angels Creek dried up in midsummer, but fortunately water was abundant in nearby rivers. A group of the county's leading citizens was organized to create a network to convey water from the Stanislaus River to the mining towns in the foothills. They were successful, and with the fruit of their effort came the start of the Union Water Company. The network was expanded, amended, added to and modified through the years, until even today it serves much of the county with not only water, but also electric power.

A professional police presence through the years amounted to little more than a one-man force, usually a sheriff or a Constable, or the "chief". It wouldn't be until well into the twentieth century that the city would require or afford additional force. The fire protection force was also long in coming, even though major fires occurred as early as 1855. Many town fires

Alexander Love's Livery and Feed stable, c. 1870

occurred since those days, the details of which can be found in a later chapter.

The "old timers" of the day, along with the area natives mingled with a few army deserters, ex-cons and a myriad of unsavory characters. Most of the citizens were law-abiding, but crime persisted through the early days. Stages were held up, lynchings persisted, and theft was a routine occurrence. People had to be very careful and cautious.

Angels Camp survived the "early days", and prospered along with some of its nearby neighbors. Most of its pioneer citizens continued to earn a living in this new territory. Yes, there were some lean years ahead, but during the era from 1885 to 1915, the mines prospered, and the town matured and became a City.

Chapter Two

GOLD EVERYWHERE

The rich surface ores, streams and veins of Angels Camp were mined for over 100 years, from 1848 on into the 1960's. The estimated total output of the area is recorded to be at least $30 million. Since no record was made of the production of gold between 1848 and 1880, this estimate could possibly be much higher.

The price to buy and sell gold was set by the U.S. government for sales prior to 1934 at $20.67 per Troy ounce. That year President Franklin D. Roosevelt declared by proclamation a devaluation of the dollar, and set the price for an ounce at $35.00. Then in the late 1960's the U.S. declared an end to what was known as the "Limited Gold Bullion Standard". Since that date, all gold has inched up in value until reaching a free-market price. The world market price has fluctuated since then, settling on the $300.00 mark, more or less, at the turn of the millennium.

By 1885 Angels Camp had become one of the major gold

mining areas in California. Surface mining of the streams and soils played out about a decade after 1848. Then, with the discovery of *veins* of gold ore, the boom was on for lode or quartz mining. Hoisting works started appearing and the change in gold mining from the pan to the underground vein or quartz mining and stamp

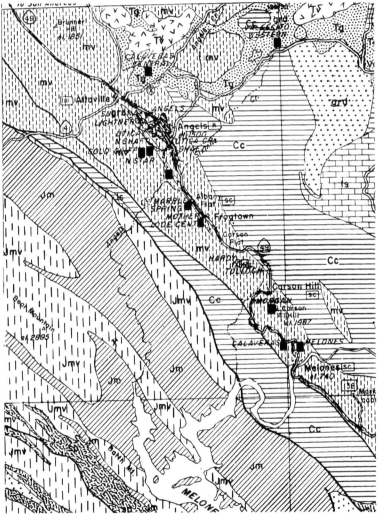

Courtesy of the State of California, Division of Mines and Geology
Geological Map of the Angels Camp-Carson Hill-Melones District.
Most mines were located in the Jurassic period meta-volcanic zone.

-10-

mill occurred. The ore bodies were scores of feet thick and hundreds of feet long. Many of the shafts reached over 3,000 feet deep from the surface.

The *UTICA MINE* was the most productive in Angels Camp. Its first name was "Invincible", and it brought great hopes and disappointments to its owners and the town. It's been said that it was once "salted" by one of its owners, James Graham Fair (see note below), in preparation of its sale. James Fair and Irwin Davis sold the claim to Attorney James T. Boyd and Judge Delos Lake of San Francisco for $30,000. It was renamed "Utica" by Judge Lake in honor of his birthplace. The new owners commenced work, and within two months were assured by the superintendent that the "salted" mine was virtually of little or no value, and that no further mining effort should be made. The owners would have been willing to sell the claim, but few offers were forthcoming. The mine was leased to a prospector, but he disappeared, and the claim was considered "abandoned". Others worked it for a few months, and they, too, moved on.

Then, one day, Robert Leeper and William B. Keyes invoked a "process" known as claim-jumping, and bonded it to D. Hunt who worked the mine for several months without much success. Leeper had come to Angels Camp in 1863, marrying Susan Stevens that same year. He built his mansion in 1882, where he and his wife lived for two years. That home, named Utica Mansion, became a celebrated landmark and earned several architectural awards. About this time, Charles D. Lane was returning from a venture in Del Norte county, and was looking for a new opportunity. Lane, being a spiritualist, took a sample of the Utica rock to a Mrs. Robinson in San Francisco. She assured him that millions were to be had from the source of that rock. He had others visit Mrs. Robinson anony-

Note: James Graham Fair was born near Belfast, Ireland, December 3, 1831, emigrated to the United States in 1843, got his start in the gold rush of California in 1849, moved to Nevada in 1860 and acquired great wealth there in silver mining. In 1881 he was elected United States Senator from Nevada, serving until 1885. He died in San Francisco on December 28, 1894.

mously with the mine's rock, and each returned with the same message, that she saw untold wealth. In November, 1884, Leeper and Keyes sold their mine and mansion to Charlie Lane who brought in other investors and bought the mine for $10,000.

Lane moved into Utica Mansion, where the residence remained the home of the Utica Mine's superintendent and subsequently Utica Power Company's managers until sold to the Pacific Gas and Electric Company in the 1940's. Thereafter it was used as a boarding house for a short time, then purchased by Kenneth Briggs who refurbished and made some alterations. Tad and Cheryl Folendorf purchased Utica Mansion in September, 1982, with the intent of operating a Bed and Breakfast house. They found that the mansion required very major restoration, so they set about to take the walls down to the studs, rewire the house, add insulation, do foundation work, add the porches and redesign the garden. They opened their Bed and Breakfast in 1988, and also provided dinners to the public for the next five years. In 1993 the Folendorfs closed their inn to the public, and continue to make the Utica Mansion, also called the Lane Mansion, their residence to this day.

For the two years between 1884 and 1886 the mine was worked faithfully, without much success. Some gold was produced, but most of the owners became disillusioned, except for Charley Lane. All of a sudden the mine began paying well after hitting a vein of immense ore yielding $200 per ton. It didn't last long, and disappointment set in again. Finally, all of the other owners sold their interest to Judge A. Hewell and Charley Lane's elder brother Andrew Lane. Things continued to drift along until in 1888 Hewell and A. Lane sold their interest for $60,000 to Alvinza Hayward (a prominent mine investor, but not to be confused with hotel owner William Hayward for whom Hayward, California was named), and pioneer lumberman Walter Hobart (who had many other interests in California: Hobart Mills, San Francisco's Hobart Building, and also other mining interests).

During the following thirty years the Utica's owners develo-

North Shaft and mill of the original twin shafts of the Utica mine

ped two deep shafts, cross-cuts, and increased mill capacity. Great management wisdom can be said of Charles D. Lane's efforts to consolidate the mines and claims in the area around the Utica.

Under his superintendency the Utica finally consisted of the Brown, Confidence, Dead Horse, Jackson, Little Nugget, Rasberry, Stickle, Gold Cliff, Madison, Utica and Washington claims. It paid off. The mills were averaging $3.60 per ton (at the old price), with small high-grade pockets frequently encountered.

Some setbacks occurred in the next few years. A tragic accident killed sixteen men. Two years later, another tragedy killed nine others. In July of 1895 a disastrous fire broke out, burning for 14 days. It became evident that the fire could not be put out by ordinary means, so the shafts were tightly bulkheaded and every available gallon of water was poured into the mine. With approximately 20,000,000 gallons each day, and for almost four days, water finally rose to extinguish the fire. Property losses were enormous, and many miners were affected by the gaseous fumes. Since the company owned a hospital, they were treated immediately in the only medical facility in town. After the fire came the tedious work of pumping the water out. It took eight weeks for the pumps and bailing skips to empty the mine. Fortunately the fire damage was confined to the small stope in which it had started. The water damage was not nearly as bad as originally thought. Although the fire caused a brief setback, the mine was back and running in short order.

The Utica continued to prosper, sinking several deep shafts and cross shafts. Their mill grew to sixty stamps. Miners were paid $3.00 a day, with helpers, shovelers and car men making $2.50. The need for additional water and power became evident.

Prior to the end of surface mining in the Angels-Carson Hill districts, the Comstock silver rush began at Virginia City, Nevada. 1859 was the year, and was the time when quartz mining in the Angels district was at a low ebb. It wasn't until the 1880's that activity in the local mines started to reach a fever pitch.

Utica Mining Company's north and south shafts

This fabulous story is covered in the next chapter.

In the main, Utica produced great riches for its owners, producing a grand total of *at least $17,000,000.00,* and was by far the most famous mine between Carson Hill and Jackson. Today's main city park of Angels Camp is located on the Utica property, and is the namesake of this fabulous gold producing mine. The entrance arch of the park is now formed by two skips that were used to traverse the shafts of the mine. The Utica mine was one of the most successful mines on the Mother Lode for over 30 years, but toward the latter part of the year 1916, it became more costly to mine the ore than it was bringing in income. On December 25th of that year, the remaining 100 men were paid off, and the Utica mine ceased operating forever.

The *STICKLE MINE* was founded and developed by George Stickle in 1852. He kept it active during the 1860's. In 1871 it had been developed to a depth of 240 feet and was equipped with a 10-stamp mill. It later was sold to Mr. F. K. Bechtel of San Francisco, who built a 20 stamp mill in 1885. After just nine days of operation the mine yielded over $14.00 per ton. This mine, too, had a major fire, causing over $100,000 damage. Charles Lane's son, Thomas, was superintendent at the time, and was given great credit for managing the fire without having to flood the mine. The Stickle Mine proved to be one of the most enduring, and one of the richest in the area, and finally joined the Utica family of mines. The headframe of the Stickle Mine was located about 100 feet up the hill behind the Forty-Niner auto dealership on Main Street.

The *GOLD CLIFF MINE* lies a half mile west of the Utica Mine on what is known as the "main spur:" of the Mother Lode. It was discovered in 1879 by pioneers of Angels Camp, Cogswell and Dolan. These two men prospected the surface of their claim, took out $8,000, and sold their claim to Captain Drake. He, in turn sold to Charles Nickerson who permitted idleness until bonded by Mssrs. Shepman, Gerrard, then Charles D. Lane. Familiar names?

Stickle mill, located where Angels Camp power house is now Situated. Note the Utica "cross shaft" in the right background, which became one of the two working shafts along with the Stickle shaft for the consolidated Utica system.

Yes, the Gold Cliff fell under the management of the Utica Mining Company in 1884. It became a consolidation of six claims with shafts worked to the 2,700 foot level. The total of *$2,834,000.00* in gold was produced at the Gold Cliff during the period up to 1920 when the mine closed for good. This closing meant that the "family" of mines being operated by the Utica Mining Company also came to a close since the Gold Cliff was the last to pay a profit.

The *MADISON MINE* (also called the Matson Mine) was adjoining the Gold Cliff to the south. Its founder, James Madison, erected a five-stamp mill in 1883, one of the most modern and best equipped in the state. It grew to forty stamps and contained four Tullock and twelve Frue concentrators. He was fortunate from the outset since the mine paid handsomely. Charles D. Lane purchased the Madison mine, and included it in the Utica Mine consolidated operation.

The Madison mine's mill, foreground, and just north lies the mill of the Gold Cliff mine. These mines were located on the main Mother Lode vein, 1,500 feet west of the Utica's vein.

The *LIGHTNER MINE* lies just north of the Utica Mine, and south of the Angels Mine. It was worked from the earliest days until 1857 at a depth of only 70 feet. It was idle for just under 40 years when it was reopened under new reorganization. Except for one year, 1910, the mine was operated continuously from 1896 until shut down in 1915, yielding roughly 500,000 tons of ore, worked in a 60 stamp mill, and bringing more than $3,000,000 to its owners.

The Bennett, Lindsay, Suffolk, Excelsior and El Dorado mines lay to the north of the Gold Cliff. To the north of the Utica, Lightner and Angels claims lies the Doc Hill Mine, successfully operated by the Angels Quartz Mining Company. Other mines in the area, such as the Uno, Dead Horse, Great Western, Bovee, West End, Confidence, Crystal, and many others played an important part in the development of Angels Camp's mining. The region from the Stanislaus River north to Fourth Crossing contains literally several hundred claims. Many of them were not worked beyond an initial effort.

The Stickle Mine, one of the earliest claims, was located just south of the Utica south shaft. During the first three decades of its existence it was an "on again, off again" operation, and didn't create great riches for its owners until after it joined the consolidation of the Utica group. It then became one of the two entries – along with the Cross Shaft – of the Utica consolidated mine.

The hoisting works or headframe of the Stickle Mine, located just a few feet south of the Suburu auto dealership. After consolidation of the Stickle and the Utica, and the abandonment of the two old Utica shafts, the Stickle and the Cross Shafts became the two working entries into the mine.

Chapter Three

WATER and POWER

Since Angels Camp was "born" to be a mining camp, it would become necessary to have water available, and lots of it. The first ten years of mining consisted of washing the soils and streambeds. This would require considerable water. Another technique used for the extraction of gold from placer deposits – or gold laden deep sand, gravel and soil – is the hydraulic method of mining, using high-pressure streams of water to wash away a hill or ledge. This would require enormous amounts of water. When an area such as Angels Camp became more and more developed with the volumes of deep ores, water in the millions of gallons would be called upon, sometimes over a very short period of time.

The natural creeks of Angels Camp supplied adequate water during the first thirty years of mining. Yes, almost all of those creeks dried up in the late summer and fall months, but there was usually water to be had most of the year from somewhere. As the mining industry grew into the 1880's, it appeared to the leading citizens that something major had to be done to bring large quantities of water to the area. And since the Utica Mining Company was the leading enterprise requiring that water, the task of bringing it to Angels Camp fell upon them.

In 1887 the Utica Mining Company purchased the Union Water Company which had twenty miles of ditch bringing water from the headwaters of the Stanislaus River in Alpine County, to

Just a few feet of the over-twenty miles of high Sierra flume that carries water from the Stanislaus headwaters to be distributed to downstream users such as Angels Camp for both power and domestic use.

the Murphys area. The following year, 1888, the Utica Mining Company made extensive repairs and improvements to these facilities, primarily in Silver Valley. Again, in 1889, water got so low they had to close the mines that fall. Utica immediately set out to build Ross Reservoir, located on French Gulch Road just west of Murphys. There continued to be a shortage of water for year-round operation, so Ross Reservoir was enlarged in 1892.

These newly acquired water holdings also allowed the Utica Mining Company to build one of the first hydroelectric power plants in California. Four Pelton wheels were installed at the Angels Camp powerhouse to power the Utica's mining machinery. Then, again, in the mid-1890's plans were made to construct a generating plant at Murphys. Water was available there, and the electricity could be transmitted to Angels Camp. The location would be a mile and a half east of Murphys on Angels Creek. It was originally designed to supply electricity for lights only. A Pelton wheel powered the Westinghouse alternator, producing 750 kilowatts. It went on line in 1899, and was transmitted at 2,500 volts eight and a half miles to Angels Camp. This venture was so successful that the capacity of the generation plant was increased in just four years. The demand for additional power required that the capacity be increased to two 750-kilowatt alternators. This new electrical generation was accomplished by the Utica Power Company, a wholly owned subsidiary of the Utica Mining Company

In 1910 the Utica Reservoir was built. Further, in 1927-28, both Spicer reservoir on Highland Creek, and Hunter reservoir near Avery were built. But, prior to the introduction of electric power in 1897 and 1902, *water* was the direct source of power by means of the wheel, Pelton and otherwise.

It was intended that the Murphys and Angels powerhouses be built to generate power for the Utica, Lightner and Gold Cliff mines only. However, the power plants were generating a surplus so it was used to power not only some of the other mines, but also the city of Angels Camp. Additional surplus was fed into the lines of the Standard Electric Company to serve San Andreas, Mokelumne Hill, Jackson, Amador City, Sutter Creek and other area cities. In 1946 the hydroelectric system, including its water rights, flumes, reservoirs and ditches still owned by the Hobart Estate, was sold and came under the ownership of the Pacific Gas and Electric Company. Subsequently, some of the water rights were reserved by the Union Public Utilities District to provide water service to Murphys, Vallecito, Red Hill Road, and Carson Hill , and continue to be held by the UPUD to this day.

Water and electrical generation in the North Fork system continued under the competent management of PG&E for over 50 years. In the mid-1990's PG&E let it be known that they preferred to divest themselves of their water and power generating facilities. At the same time, a local group proposed purchasing the facilities. It became apparent immediately that a value or selling price for such a complicated operation would be difficult to determine. Negotiation between this group and PG&E, with a federal commission overview, finally achieved agreement. The upper portion of the system, including the high-country reservoirs, delivery creeks and flumes and ditches, was purchased by the Northern California Power Authority. The lower portion was purchased by the Utica Power Authority. The lower portion consisted of the new tunnel connection with Hunter Reservoir, on through the delivery system to Murphys complex, Angels Creek and beyond to Ross Reservoir and Angels Camp (for both water and power generation). The UPA was a joint effort of three entities, the UPUD (Murphys, Vallecito, Red Hill and Carson Hill water interests), the City of Angels Camp, and the Calaveras County Water District. Each of these entities had two representative votes, for a total of six votes. Subsequent squabbles between the parties occurred, but by this date, the operation appears to be operating smoothly and successfully.

The water delivery to Angels Camp at the millennium is the envy of most cities. Water quality is close to perfect, and water pressure is delivered at over 100 ppi., all gravity created pressure. The water mains and other infrastructure are replaced on a regular basis. The delivery capacity is being doubled, due to an expanded population.

Some very important people are responsible for building, operating and maintaining these facilities over the years. Undoubtedly, Charlie Lane would be a major player, being the

Utica Mine Superintendent, and an owner. Many, many would be building and maintaining the system during the first part of the twentieth century, including Al Wilson, Ephraim Cutting, Jo Prieg, W. Thomas, W. Kiefer, Morris Cohen, Isaac Levi, Al Gianelli, Jack Twisselman, Elton Dorrah, Billy Lagomarsino and John Fletcher. In the latter years, Oliver Garcia, Loren Whittle, Marshall Nichols, and Al Ponce played a major part.

In 1984 the domestic water system was sold by PG&E to several entities, one of which was the City of Angels Camp. The city now operates the system along with the sewer system that was mandated by the state during the mid-1900's.

Al Gianelli poses at the Utica Power Company's Generator at the original "old" powerhouse in Murphys.

Power for the electrical generating plants, the mine's hoisting machinery, and the stamp mills (which crushed the ore), came about as the result of water, in one form or another. The water could be a low-pressure flow of water, a high-pressure flow of water, or it could be vaporized water, or steam. All three of these were used in the mines, sometimes together, sometimes as backup to the other, but always used for driving the machinery of the mines. Always, that is, until the development of electric power. But, then again, water was used to drive the electrical generating machinery, so it was water that was "king", and more and more was needed with every passing day.

The early water wheels were of the overshot design, using large amounts of relatively low pressure water. Then it was found that by using a small quantity of water at a high pressure on an undershot wheel, a much more efficient power source was obtained, and with a far higher rate of revolution. The Pelton Wheel was invented, refined, tested, was constantly observed until it became a highly efficient tool to move machinery. The view, below, illustrates the high-pressure nozzle in the foreground.

The Pelton Wheel

A magnificent Pelton wheel is on display at the Angels Museum, outdoors at the lower level.

In 1896 a Pelton wheel was installed for power on the new Cross shaft. The Pelton-driven water power drove the hoisting machinery on the Cross shaft for approximately 18 years until the Utica mining operations concluded.

Chapter Four

SCHOOLS and CHURCHES

SCHOOLS

From 1848 to 1854 there was no school in Angels Camp. Civic mindedness was one of the attributes of the forty-niner. Joseph Hill spearheaded the effort to open an elementary school, rented a room in one of Bennager Rasberry's buildings, and hired John Brickell as the teacher. Hill had just arrived at Slab Ranch ("East" Altaville) in 1854, with his wife and four children, and immediately saw the need to organize a public school. He provided free room and board to John Brickell in return for transporting the Slab Ranch children safely to school. This was Angels Camp's first school. During the first days of the Gold Rush, very few miners had a wife with them, let alone their children. As the years went by, the enrollment of schools increased, and additional classrooms were needed.

The second school, but first school *house*, was built just several blocks up the hill, and was known as the Purdyville School. Located on South Summit Street in the area near the Stickle Mine's hoist, and behind what was then the mortuary facility, this school quickly grew to 140 pupils. Oddly enough, by 1870 the school had grown by just a handful of students. When the mining activity picked up in the 70's and 80's those figures doubled. Due to this growth, classes for the lower grades were moved to rooms in the Masonic Hall. By the end of the century this school's enrollment was bursting at the seams. Another schoolhouse was sorely needed.

Purdyville School, Angels Camp's first schoolhouse was located just north of 1222 South Summit. It burned during the first decade of the 20th century. A companion building built at 1222 was both a Methodist church and school, and operated until it was turned into "Sams Place", a miners' rooming, boarding and watering place. It still stands today serving as a private residence.

Some of the early teachers were John Brickell, W. J. Brockway, W. M. Durham, John Hancock, Edward Leonard, William Lombardi, Newell, Peachy, William Redding, Frank Wells, and his father J. H. Wells. In 1857 the following 49 pupils were reported enrolled: James Boote, Eliza Brodie, Marion Bush, James Childers, Thornton Childers, John Fletcher, Emma Foreman, Rhoda Foreman, Albert Frazier, David Gardiner, Lucy

Green, Albert Hill, Henry Hill, Mary Hill, Lucretia Hill, William Jackson, Mary Lake, Frank Lertora, John Lindsay, Elizabeth Love, Robert Love, Daniel Miller, Henry Miller, William Newman, James Nicholson, Alice Reddick, John Reddick, Charles Reeves, Grace Richards, Elizabeth Richardson, Vihini Risi, Sarah Rollin, William Rose, Frederick Spellner, Madge Spellner, James Spink, Samual Spink, Polly Talbot, Isabel Tappen, Jeanette Tarbot, Cornelia Thomas, Mary Thomas, Sara Underhill, Elisha Waterman, Lucy Waterman, Mary Waterman, William Waterman, Isabella Welch, and Susan Wise.

Angels Camp's "new" two story elementary school, built in 1899 on Finnegan Lane. It boasted having eight classrooms, plus a library/music room. This school served well from 1899 until Mark Twain School was built 1950.

At a cost of $10,000, a new elementary school was built on Finnegan Lane in 1899. It was two stories high, and consisted of an office, eight schoolrooms, a library/music room and furnace room. The furnace room was a favorite hangout on cold and rainy days. All of the children walked to school, and classes started at nine. When this new school opened Angels Camp was abuzzing,

Third and fourth grade students at the Finnegan Lane school. They are (top row) Louise Crespi, Fred Kreth, uk, Bill Airola, Wilbur Eberhardt, Robert Cooper, Owen Riley, Fred Canepa, uk, Donald Faull, Madeline "Tutu" Revelino.   Second row, June Soracco, Elaine Miladinovich, Betty Pettit, Dolores Castle, Mae Slavazza, (teacher) Rose McCauley, Helen Riley, Barbara Lemue, Roseline Kathan.   Third row, Wilford Kathan, Albert Baratono, Frank Rolleri, Jim Tarbat, uk, uk, Dick Rolleri, Jack Rodman. Front row, Albert Pecchenino, Donald Fletcher, Johnny Miller, George Segale. uk=unknown. Class picture in 1933.

mines and stamp mills were running around the clock, seven days a week. The Finnegan Lane schoolhouse was in continuous use until 1950, when the Angels and Altaville districts joined and became the Mark Twain Elementary School.

Going back to the year 1859, one additional "Angels Camp" Elementary school was built in Altaville. Although it was not in the city limits, it was officially formed as a part of the Angels District. The *San Andreas Independent* said, "…it stands upon a beautiful natural eminence and presents quite a pleasing ornament as well as a useful appendage to the town." The building was a very attractive structure, built of brick made in a local kiln, and was 24' x 36'. Funds to construct the school were raised by holding a dance in the Billiard Saloon of the Prince and Garabardi Building.

The school also served as a center for the town's activities. A second wooden schoolhouse was added close by the brick structure, and served the upper grade students. In 1950 the two buildings were closed when Altaville became a part of the Mark Twain School District. The wooden building was removed, and the brick schoolhouse relocated closer to Main Street and restored under the sponsorship of the Calaveras County Historical Society. It has become State Historical Landmark No. 499, and is listed in the National Registry of Historic Places.

In the meantime those students that desired to continue on to high school would have to attend classes in one of the larger cities, such as Stockton, Sacramento or elsewhere. Finally, in 1904, the Calaveras County Union High School District was established, but the county fathers located the first high school in San Andreas. Well, the citizens of Angels Camp were furious. In less than a year Angels Camp residents formed a high school district of their own, voted in a bond issue, and started construction of their own high school to be known as Bret Harte Union High School. It was located on Stanislaus Street in the Altaville area, its first principal being Lucius D. McKinley. The two high schools have been avid rivals ever since.

This new high school was not a picture of beauty, but it was furnished with state-of-the-art equipment for its three departments, academic, scientific and commercial. As enrollments increased, new classrooms were added. Two courses were offered – a four-year college preparatory, and a two-year commercial course. The first graduates of the two-year course were Eva Gazzola and Lizzie Hart. The first graduates of the four-year

Angels Camp's first High School, built in 1906. It was not a picture of beauty being bat'n'board, but all equipment, lab materials and facilities were the best money could buy.

This photo was taken in 1908. The schoolhouse was greatly expanded and improved, and became much more attractive.

academic program were Gertrude Carlow, Kate Cutler, Annie Harp, Frank McClory and Rebekah Gardner.

In the early years at Bret Harte, the prime sport was baseball. Opposing teams were Calaveras High and Tuolumne County High School. The team's outstanding players in 1910 were Virgil Airola, Ben Carlow, George Moore, Jerome Porter, Norman Smith and Fred Schwartz. Basketball was also a "league" sport, but did not get going for several years, until experienced coaches and a larger team membership could come into play. Football was not played until 1929. Some players during that year were Oliver Bernasconi, Earl Brunner, Guy Castle, Sam Giovenetti, Ray Lagomarsino Earl Lewis, Florin McAfee, Tom McClure, Paul McNutt, and Tom Rolleri. The coach was Harry Auten, the geometry and music teacher.

Girl's organized sports were not very active during the early years. The school Annual in 1910 showed a picture of the girls basketball team, under a heading of "Jokes". By 1925, the girl's baseball team received much more respect. Coached by Jesse Jones, that team included Laura Black (Hutchins), Zilda Delucchi (Arthur), Phyllis Lewis (Pickup), Annie Lombardi (Voitich), Earline Oneto (Young), Amelia Paredes, Carrie Paredes, Irene Peirano, and Dorothy Ratkovich (Soracco). Over the years, girl's teams improved. By 1980 Bret Harte was riding high. Both the girls basketball and volleyball teams were not only the Mother Lode League's winners, but both went on to achieve further notoriety. The 1984-85 boys varsity basketball team went all the way to Oakland-Alameda County Arena, vying for the Division IV Northern California Championship. They fell just two points short of continuing on for the State Championship. Some of those team members were Tim Lilly, Rich Hogan, Jim Kern, Keith Rakoncza, Jim Hecker, Roland Wheeler and Ron Loomis, and coached by Rich Cathcart, with Hal Clements as Athletic Director.

During the early years of the first high school, students living in the outlying areas of the district had difficulty getting to school. Finally, in 1923, John Carley was contracted by the school to bring students in from district areas. Those from further outlying towns had to attend Calaveras High School, and physically drove within a block of Bret Harte High School on their way to San Andreas.

(Above) A brand new Bret Harte High School, completed in 1926.

(Below) A four-photo panorama of Murphys Grade Road looking directly at the site of the "new" high school campus. Note the girls gymnasium in left distance of right panel.

In the 1920's, the high school was becoming inadequate. The voters approved a $60,000 bond issue, and a new high school was built on Main Street in Altaville. Five acres of land were purchased, construction began, and by mid-year 1926 the new high school was completed. It grew, and matured, and grew some more until a major change in the school districts of the county occurred in the mid-1970s.

The entire county was re-districted, lines generally drawn down an east-west boundary that divided the county into a north and a south district. Calaveras High School would draw its pupils from the north half of the county, and Bret Harte High School would draw from the south half. This meant that students would no longer "drive by" Bret Harte on the way to Calaveras from areas such as Avery and Arnold, a much more sensible plan. This plan was becoming an obvious necessity, but would require a major effort of a county-wide citizen panel to spearhead such a major change. The "yes" vote to make this change was over-whelming.

The buildings at the Main Street high school had become inadequate by 1975. The Board of Education brought in a new principal and superintendent, John Provart. He accomplished wonders by creating a new high school campus behind (and east of) the Main Street building, which was closed to classes in 1977. The new campus was expanded, the old boys gymnasium was renovated and given over exclusively to the girls, and a new gym

was built to house the boys. The new campus was built entirely on the old football field, which meant that a new field had to be built. The old football bleachers still sit on the hillside, a reminder of those years past. New bleachers were built, lights were erected, and a magnificent track was installed around the new football field. A baseball diamond, soccer field and practice field were also added. Further expansion occurred in 1998, when the campus was greatly enlarged to include several acres directly across Murphys Grade Road from the school. A student parking lot was constructed, and plans are afoot for a swimming complex and tennis courts.

Today's Bret Harte High School has achieved superior academic ranking, and is fielding sport teams that are competitive throughout the area. The teaching and administrative staff, under the direction of Superintendent Joseph Wilimek and Principals Milt Goodrich, John Provart, Bob Bach, Ron Lewis, Jan Edwards and Catherine Sargent, have created an academic program and environment that is enviable.

The Main Street high school building that had been vacated for class instruction was alleged to have burned to the ground at the hands of two teen-aged arsonists. The remains were demolished and the land lay idle for ten years. Almost immediately after the fire it was decided that a performing arts center or a sports/swimming complex should be built, but those plans would be put on hold until funds could be raised. Finally, an insurance money squabble was settled, priorities were made, plans were drawn, and construction of a performing arts center was started on September 5, 2000. It was the intention of the school Board that the facility be used not only for school functions, but also some community functions.

CHURCHES

The early missionaries that came to Angels Camp found that they were confronted with many problems that were difficult

Left: St. Patrick's Catholic Church as it appeared in this 1938 photo. Right: St. Vasilije's Serbian Church, the oldest Serbian church west of the Mississippi River, after Caltrans moved it back.

to solve. First, most of the citizens traveled on foot or horseback, and on crude trails. Second, the ethnic origins of the people were so diverse – native Indians, soldiers, sailors, farmers, Negroes, Creoles, Chinese, Mormons, Australians, South Americans, Mexicans, Frenchmen, Germans, British, Dutchmen, and every other possible conceivable type. The missionaries described the town as being in distress, riddled with crime, and drinking and gambling to excess. Nevertheless, they set about to bring their missions to Angels Camp.

In 1850, Archbishop Joseph Sadoc Alemany, O.P. came to San Francisco and headed the Catholic Church's Diocese. He sent

Father Aleric to Sonora, who was to administer some of the nearby towns. Father Aleric held services in Angels Camp and urged parishioners to erect a church. It wasn't until 1854 that "a neat little wooden building with a modest steeple" was completed, and named St. Michaels. It sat on the main highway from Angels Camp to Stockton, on a parcel with an 80-foot front that also included a burial ground. Unfortunately, this small church was destroy by fire the very next year. Services were then held in the town hall. A second church was built near the Lightner Mill, and was named St. Columbo's. That church was later moved to the site of the present-day Catholic church, and was used as the church rectory.

It wasn't until 1901 that the first resident priest, Father Vaughn, would come to Angels Camp. He didn't trust the location of his church, fearing it was sitting on unstable, honeycombed land, so he set about to build another new church and parsonage. One of his parishioners, James V. Coleman, donated a lot, and subscribed $100 a month until the buildings were paid for. It was named St. Patrick's Roman Catholic Church, and was dedicated by Father Alemany. This facility served well for eighty years, but was deemed too small. It was torn down in 1981, and an entirely new church and hall were built. In addition to the church, an Education Building was built along with the church. It was needed for social events, a preschool, and for a catechism school. This construction came about largely with funds from the Crespi family. The 100th anniversary will be marked with a celebration in 2001.

On February 2, 1859, a group of gentlemen organized for the purpose of establishing the Methodist Episcopal Church. Within a few months, citizens gathered to select a site. Newspaper accounts reported that a new Methodist Church was being built in "a pleasant location" in Altaville, and that it would accommodate 250 persons.

In 1909, the many Serbians who lived in Angels Camp, and especially in the Purdyville area, wanted a church of their own. By

September 4th of that year, construction began on their Orthodox Church. It was located at the northern intersection of what is now know as Bret Harte and Main Streets, on a lot 80' x 100'. The first services were held in 1910, and the first trustees were John Krzich, Pete S. Grgwrevich and John M. Bronzich. They named their church Saint Vasilije's Serbian Orthodox Church. It sat in that location until the 1930's, when the State Department of Transportation (highway's CalTrans) required that since Saint Vasilije's was sitting in the middle of a planned new highway that it had to be moved a few feet back. CalTrans moved the facility to accommodate the new highway.

Students of Christian Science were meeting in Murphys in 1934 for the purpose of organizing a local Christian Science Society. They moved their meetings to Vallecito, but finally decided to purchase a piece of property in Angels Camp. Because of WWII, building plans were put on hold. On February 1, 1947, the Society rented a building in Angels Camp for meetings, and plans were again made to build their church. In early 1948 construction was started, and on Wednesday evening, February 16, 1949, the first services were held in the new church, which then became known as the First Church of Christ, Scientist, Angels Camp, but is now known as the Christian Science Society. The building was "publicly consecrated to God" on June 5, 1949, with the announcement that "all indebtedness incidental to the building had been paid".

The Angels Camp Faith Chapel Assembly of God held its first services on December 12, 1948. Reverend Kenneth Brown officiated at that service. It's located in the Purdyville area. Angels Camp's First Baptist Church can be found on the way to the old train station on Depot Road, next door to the Christian Science Society. The Union Congregational Church is on Main Street in the downtown area, while Seventh-day Adventist Church is on Main Street a mile north in Altaville. Behind the high school's athletic fields lies the Church of The Nazarene, on Murphys Grade Road. The newest church, just completed four months prior to the millennium is the Foothill Community Church, located on Glory Hole Road (or Whittle Road). Rounding out the area churches is the Iglesia Apostolica De La Fe En Cristo Jesus, situated on Main Street in the southern extreme of the city.

Chapter Five

FIRE and POLICE

Fires have played a major role in the history and development of Angels Camp. The first big fire occurred in 1855, just as the town was getting its start. The whole town burned. Almost all of the structures were made of wood, many were simply canvas. At that time there was no fire department, not even a pumper or hose truck. The only source for putting out a town fire was the bucket brigade. Everyone pitched in to douse a fire. An adequate water supply played a big part, naturally, and there was no assurance that water would be available in the early days. During late summer and the fall seasons, most of the creeks became dry, leaving little water to douse a fire.

The 1855 fire leveled the entire town from Angels Creek to the Catholic church. Many structures were rebuilt from local lava rock and stones, with iron doors and shutters. Some roofs were layered with sand or dirt. Then, again in 1856, fire burned a section of town between two fireproof buildings. In 1885 a fire starting in the Cosgrove Hotel burned 15 businesses on both sides of Main

Main Street, Angels Camp, shortly after the fire of 1885. The Angels Hotel is on the right.

Street, plus all of Chinatown. Around the turn-of-the-century high pressure water became available at the Utica Mine. Prior to city incorporation, the Utica made this pressurized water available for downtown firefighting in the form of stationary nozzles. Some called them "Giants', and some called them "Giant Brodies. They were unique in that they were connected directly to the water mains without the use of hoses. They had a double swivel, and were invented by a Mr. Brodie, a local mine engineer. A few years later the townspeople raised enough money to buy two "hose carts". They were manned by two fire companies, the "Utica" and the "Eureka". One of these carts was stationed at the bridge on Main Street, and was swept down the creek in the flood of 1909. You can pay a visit to the Angels Camp main fire house and see one of these "hose carts", plus a fabulous historical collection of pictures, facts, and artifacts collected mainly by the fire department's longtime historian, Mr. Fenton Bolton.

Another fire in September, 1931, burned the wooden Commercial Hotel, along with six businesses. This hotel was immediately rebuilt with fireproof materials. It was renamed the Bazinett Hotel, and since renamed the Utica Hotel. It still stands today. Then, seven years later a third major hotel fire burned Olivia Rolleri's Calaveras Hotel and eight businesses. It was never rebuilt. The Visitor's Bureau and parking facility now sit in its location. By the following February, 1939, fire hydrants were installed in the city for the first time. Then, in 1941, the Woods Hall and Opera House building burned to the ground. It contained several lodge rooms, some stores, and the most popular dance hall in town. It was a huge loss in those pre-TV days. That site first housed the Scribner-Matthews Store, the Rasmussen Store, and the first Wells Fargo Office. Walter Valente's Barber Shop was burned. Walter says, "...but I saved the chair". He moved his shop up the street and continued barbering for another year.

The town of Angels Camp was incorporated into a city in 1912. In that same year, on August 20th, the Fire Department was formalized. It had always been a volunteer operation, and continued to be so. The first Fire Chief selected was Joe Zwinge. It wasn't until May 5, 1917, that the city purchased its first fire engine, a double-tank chemical engine. The price was $1,250.00, the make was American LaFrance and the mounting was a Ford truck chasis.

The second fire truck joined the department in 1925, and was also an American LaFrance chemical engine. This time it was on a Dodge truck chasis. It still sits proudly in the Fire Department Museum located at the central fire station. The year 1935 was a big one for the department. It was reorganized that year with five Commissioners: C. H. Wood, A. C. Wilson, Dr. G. F. Pache, L. Monteverde, and Harry Barden, Secretary. Jack Twissleman was appointed Chief. His assistants were A. S. Pecchenino, Romie Rolleri, and Jack Manuel. Other members were L. Werle, James

-41-

Oneto, F. R. Adams, Jack Valente, W. J. Raggio, John LeMue, Jack White, Joe Carley, Joe Baratono, Wilbur Lillie, Louis Vettorazzi, James Malespina, W. B. Siegel, John Lamb, with Louis Dorrah as Treasurer, and E. A. Walker as Secretary.

That same year, seven new "Giant Brodies" were installed on Main Street, and the department began its annual summer program for burning the vacant lots around the city. At that time the membership of the fire department was large enough to take on this huge undertaking. This volunteer effort continued for over a half-century until it became so burdensome that its members could no longer continue. At one time during this period, the department could boast over 40 firefighters. Now, the department consists of less than 20 volunteer members, although the present firefighter is much better trained in both fire sciences and health/medical sciences. Two years later an effort was made to float a bond issue for a new fire truck and fire house. It failed by a vote of 132 to 112. Then, in '39, Chief Twissleman commenced a program to replace some of the "giants" with fire plugs. The city replaced three plugs, and the Utica Mining Company installed two "Cory Duals" on Main Street. That same year four 4" valves replaced the "giants" on Bush Street. A huge reorganization occurred on December 5, 1941, with an auxiliary membership. Jack Twissleman was reelected chief, with Moxie Folendorf as President; Vice President, Joe Carley; Secretary, James Valente; Treasurer, Louis Dorrah, Sergeant at Arms, Robert Tarbet; First Assistant Chief, John Lemue, Second Assistant Chief, Fred Wilder; and Third Assistant Chief, Joe Carley.

Four fire companies were organized. Company Number One consisted of Louis Vettorazzi as Captain, with R. M. Grexton, J. T. Lamb, and Robert Tarbat. Company Number Two consisted of Joe Carley as Captain, with E. W. Dorrah, C. A. Twisselman, and Wm. Raggio. Company Number Three consisted of W. R. Siegel as Captain, with Jack White, Ted Bird, and James Valente, and Company Number Four consisted of C. D. Follendorf as Captain, with James Oneto, A. J. Dorrah, and Earl Carley.

The new Fire Auxiliary consisted of the following members: George Cooper, Dave Dragone, George Tryon, Alvin Hogarth, Ed Leonard, Wes Thomas, Russell Dragone, Ellsworth Alford, Frank Rolleri, Jack Rolleri, Jesse Mayo, Gerald Starr, Orval Anderson, Jack Vettorazzi, Sam Johnston, Lloyd Martin, Walter Valente, Dave Rice, R. H. Dynan and Mel Zwinge.

Early in 1949 the Emerson Dual Resuscitator was purchased from L. N. Curtis and Sons. Immediately thereafter, attachments for the resuscitator were added. The medical aid crew was appointed, consisting of Clarence Castle as Captain, with Tony Zanardi, Dale Pludeman, Dave Dragone and Earl Edmiston. The year 1949 was the beginning of medical responses by the Fire Department. In 1999 the department received a total of 403 calls, with 235 of these for medical aid.

The *Roll of Fireman* is long. We salute each of these firemen, and give our thanks for the effort and time devoted to their voluntary contribution.

Adams, Frank	Hogarth, Alvin	Pache, Dr. Geo.
Airola, Tone	Hutchinson, Wm.	Quilici, James
Ardahl, Lawrence	Hutchinson, E.	Revelino,Joe
Anderson, Eugene	Jermey, Al	Rolleri, Romi
Alford, Ellsworth	Jesson, Frank	Raggio, Ernest, Jr.
Anderson, Orval	Johnson, Myron	Reid, Elmer
Beers, Herb	Jones, Harold	Raggio, James
Bernard, Waldo	Jensen, R. H.	Ramorini,Lorin
Barden, Harry	Johnston, Sam	Raggio, Peter
Baratono, Joe	Kennedy, H. A.	Reinking, George
Bohag, W. E.	Keran, Ray	Rader, Marvin
Beltramo, Albert	Loomis, George	Rolleri, John
Berg, Fran	Lamb, John	Rolleri, Frank
Bergantz. Cecil	Lemue, John	Rice, Dave
Bongard, John	Lillie, Wilbur	Sorocco,.Mel
Baratono, Barnie	Leonard, Ed	Siegel, W. B.
Bolton, Fenton	Luly, Jim	Schena, Guisto

Carley, Earl
Copello, Dave
Colendich, Nick
Cooper, Geo. P.
Cooper, Geo. W.
Carley, Joe
Carlow, Ben
Chapman, Earl
Crespi, Charles
Croshaw, Harry
Caton, Herb
Castle, Clarence
Carley, Wade
Dorrah, Louis
Devore, C. M.
Dragone, Dave
Dutil, Tony
Dillashaw, Harold
Drummond, Harold
Dragone, Russell
Dynan, R. H.
Eberhardt, Charles
Eberhardt, Wilbur
Edmiston, Earl
Errecart, Martin
Folendorf, C. D.
Feldon, George
Foppiano, Ray
Fletcher, John
Foster, Leo
Grexton, Rollie
Gualdoni, Adolf
Griffin, E. S.
Grillo, Frank

Lagomarsino, Les
Lucini, Louis
Lockhart, Bruce
LaBrenz, Ray
Mayo, Jesse Jr
Mayo, Ray
Mosner, Ernie
Malespina, James
Mercer,Robert
McNutt, Paul
Manuel, J. A.,Jr.
Micheles, D.
Morales, Tom
Modahl, Kerner
Moore, Wm.
Moller, Nels
Malespina, Mel
Mayo, Jess
Merritt,George
Minto, Vrle
Mortonsen,Niel
Marzi, Lino
Martin, Lloyd
Monteverde,
    Lawrence
Nelson, Robert
Ordway, Ed
Oneto, James
O'Connor, Ray
Pecchenino, A.S.
Popenhagen, G.
Price, G.
Pludeman, Dale
Price, Mel

Segale, Maynard
Schmidt,.Ed
Solo, Al
Supinger, Bob
Smith, Kenneth
Soracco, Roy
Stone, Charles
Starr, Gerald
Tarbat, Robert
Tennyson, Ralph
Tocalino, C.
Thomas, Wes
Twisselman, Jack
Tryon, George
Vettorazzi, Louis
Valente, Jack
Valente, James
Vierra, John
Vineyard, Carl
Vettorazzi, Louis
Valente, Walter
Wilson, A. F.
Wilson, A. C.
Werley, Lawrence
Walker, E. A.
White, Jack
Wood, C. H.
Wilder, Fred
Wein, M. A.
Wood, Harold C.
Walsh, Earl
Winters, Vernon
Zwinge, Joe
Zwinge, Mel
Zanardi, Tony

An up-to-date listing of current and recent members of the department would increase the size of the listing by several dozen names. We hope to include those names in a future printing.

THE BIG SIX FIRES - The City of Angels Camp has experienced several horrendous fires over the years. The first, a devastating wipe-out of the entire town in 1855 (and again the following year) is mentioned above. Everything burned from Angels Creek to the Catholic church. At that time the "buildings" were built of either wood or canvas. Since both burn readily, and since no viable fire-fighting organization or equipment existed to douse a fire, that fire spread quickly, and was total and complete. Several "fireproof" buildings had been built prior to the '56 fire, which was stopped between two of these buildings.

The 1885 fire was a major conflagration. The Angels Hotel had been built of stone, and did not burn. The Cosgrove Hotel, a wooden structure, burned to the ground along with many downtown businesses and most homes on Birds Way.

The next big fire occurred in 1931, when the Commercial Hotel was destroyed. The ability of the town and its citizens to put out great fires was still non-existant. Being of wood construction, the hotel burned to the ground. It was located on the west side of Main Street, just three buildings north of Finnegan Lane. Owners got busy immediately, and rebuilt the hostelry, this time of reinforced concrete. They called it the Bazinett Hotel. It stands today, mostly vacant and run-down, and now named the Utica Hotel.

Another big hotel in downtown, the 54-room Calaveras Hotel, burned beyond repair, in December, 1938. Walter Valente described the nature of the fire. "It was in the middle of the night, the smoke and flames went straight up into the sky, no wind, no buffing, just straight up high into the air." Ironically, plans were on the table to install high-pressure water hydrants on Main Street in the following year. This hotel, too, was located on the west side

On a cold December night in 1938, fire totally destroyed Grandma Rolleri's Calaveras Hotel, a much revered landmark, and home to many families and visitors in Angels Camp. Compare this photo to the picture on page 84.

of Main Street, in the second block from the creek. The new Visitors Bureau and Center, with its parking facility, is now located on the site. One of Angels Camp's most famous citizens, Olivia Rolleri, ran the hotel for over 35 years. It was never rebuilt.

The next conflagration occurred on August 1, 1979, on Main Street, high on the hill. Not a hotel this time, but the lumber yard of the Calaveras Lumber Company. It was a virtual total loss. The main thrust of the fire was a brand new warehouse, built just

Upper photo, next page: Calaveras Lumber's warehouse goes up in flame on August 1, 1979. The four white puffs above the roof, and the white background inside the building, are all pure, hot flame.   *Courtesy of Michael Fullaway*
Lower photo: Bret Harte High School, still burning after three hours, on July 14, 1994. The building burned further, and was a total loss. It was fully insured.   *Courtesy of Norma J. Manners*

three years prior to the fire. It had been filled with finish lumber and merchandise. Other materials were stored throughout the inside and outside of the building. It was all burned to the ground. Mike Fullaway, Calaveras Lumber's owner, said the fire was fast and swift, taking exactly seven minutes from start to finish. The office was destroyed, with all of its contents. He went on to say, "conditions were ideal for a fire, due to four days of 100-plus degree weather, with only 3 to 4 percent humidity." After a full investigation, CDF concluded that it started from an unattended lit cigarette. The company has a very strict "No Smoking" policy. Several stacks of lumber in the yard, and a small hardware store did not burn.

Then, in the early morning hours of July 14, 1994, Angels Camp's largest building burned to the ground. This was the Bret Harte High School's no-longer-used-for-classes main building built in 1925-26. It was partially occupied by the County Office of Education, and was used mainly for the high school's storage. Some meeting rooms were used as a Senior Center, but none of the rooms in the entire facility was used or occupied by the high school for classes. The "new" (3rd) high school had been built several years prior to the fire, just east of its predecessor. Although construction is not completed at this writing, a performing arts auditorium is expected to open in late 2001.

Police Affairs

Little police presence was apparent during the early days of Angels Camp, and the criminal records of the citizenry were not chronicled until newspapers came onto the scene. There was plenty of crime, mostly theft, but during the first years of the town this crime was usually dealt with, swiftly and summarily.

With the advent of California's statehood, and the establishment of Calaveras County came the duly elected sheriff and his deputies, and the court's constables. The services of both of these offices slowly came to the town. Yes, stages were held up

Charles Bolton, alias Black Bart at the time of his arrest in 1883.

in those days, but not in the Angels Camp city area. One of the county's most notorious stage robbers, Black Bart, was active just outside of the area, as was Joaquin Murietta.

But the main activity of the Chief was to walk the streets, checking businesses and making sure doors were locked, and providing an aire of security among the townspeople. He had to haul the drunks and lawbreakers off to jail. The city jail was a simple stone building on Birds Way. Some considered a stay there worse than being hanged.

The first officer in memory was Constable Jerome O'Connor who held the ominous nickname of Hawk shaw. This was Never mentioned to his face. He served in that capacity until his death in the 1930's. Mel Zwinge replaced O'Connor as Constable. The town had become an incorporated city a few years prior, and was in need of a police office, so six years after his appointment as Constable, Mel was also appointed Chief of Police. A night-officer also served to assist the Chief. That position was filled by Johnnie Lamb, who assumed the post of Chief of Police when Mel Zwinge quit in 1954. After Lamb's service came Joe Spinelli who was the first Chief to initiate the use of police radio, and was responsible for the first real enforcement of a "curfew". He was also the Chief when, during the first week of June, 1957, the annual "Gypsy Tour" brought about 5,000 motorcyclists to Angels Camp. This deluge of people was the first to decent upon the city, and required additional help. At that time, a young and personable officer had joined the ranks of the county sheriff. His name was George Baratono. George assisted throughout this event, which was not a city event, but much of the activity, parades and revelry happened in the city. The main events were held at the fairgrounds in Frogtown, about three miles south of the city limits. Then, in 1959, Floyd Segale was appointed Chief of Police, and served well for three years. He retained the office of Constable, but resigned his office of Chief to take on another supervisorial position at a Copperopolis asbestos mine.

In 1962, long-time resident of Angels Camp George Baratono became its Chief of Police. His philosophy was, "lets try to keep them from committing crimes – crime prevention. If we can stop them, let's do it." He was very successful as Chief, primarily because he felt that his official presence on the streets was a deterrent to crime rather than jailing them. If they were from out of town and had money, he'd put them up in a hotel for the night. "What good was it going to do to throw them in jail," said Baratono.

He also remembers the Jumping Frog Jubilee of "71. It was estimated that 100,000 people attended that fair (some have estimated as low as 60,000), and roughly 2,000 motorcyclists roared into town. The town was overwhelmed. Sheriff Russell Leach's 30 deputies were insufficient to handle the crowds. Mutual aid was requested, and 100 officers responded from San Joaquin, Stanislaus, Sacramento, Tuolumne, Amador and Alpine Counties, as well as Stockton, Modesto, Tracy, Lodi, Manteca and Ripon Police. Motorcyclists "cruised" up and down the city streets, and parked 20 deep around the local bars. Fortunately, crime within the city was minimal.

George loved the kids, and they love him. He would never take a kid to jail, but would take them home to their parents. Most parents would discipline their children, which Baratono preferred to have happen. He was a single-man police force, which left him no back-up. However, he established a volunteer police reserved to be used in emergencies.

The most notorious robber in Calaveras County was Black Bart, mentioned above. His holdup record was never proved, because he pleaded guilty to his accusations. Was it 27 or 28? That's enough robberies to keep a man busy for some time. He did not contest the charges against him, and was sentenced to six years in San Quentin. It is thought that his first holdup occurred on July 26, 1875. Almost all of his holdups were against Wells Fargo Stages. He never killed any of his victims, but his haul of gold amalgam and gold coins amounted to approximately $4 to $5,000 on many occasions. Wells Fargo was hit hard by Black Bart, and they brought in special agents and investigators to bring him to justice. His holdups never occurred in the city, but the Angels Camp Wells Fargo agent was always involved in investigations. Most of Black Barts holdups were perpetrated in the Copperopolis area at Funk Hill.

Black Bart was not the only stage robber in the area. The first recorded holdup occurred on February 17, 1857, just a mile west of Murphys. Hundreds of stages were robbed during the 1870 to 1885 period. In Calaveras, the stages operating over Funk Hill on the Sonora-Copperopolis-Milton Road were most often hit. "Big Mitch" Ratovich, "Little Mitch" Brown, "Old Joaquin" Savage, and Ramon Ruiz were the most common names mentioned. A one-eyed amateur was poor and in need of some quick cash, so he disguised himself and held up a stage. He was apprehended immediately because it was reported that the bandit wore a flour sack as a mask, with a hole cut for only one eye. There was only one one-eyed local, who was taken into custody by Sheriff Thorn. Crime against Wells Fargo & Co. over the 1870-85 period cost the company almost a million dollars.

Crime during the last hundred years in Angels Camp has been remarkably quiet. Perhaps the most dramatic incident, a shooting, turned out to be more of an accident than a crime. Arson has probably been the most costly crime committed during the century. Our police force concerns itself mostly with traffic problems and misdemeanor offenses. The citizens of Angels Camp have been model citizens, and are able to live in a quiet, peaceful town.

Chapter Six

STAGES, TRAINS and BUSES

The early transportation in and out of Angels Camp consisted of horseback, buggy, wagon and stage. At the outset there were no roads, and there were few trails, including those established by the indigenous populace. When the gold rush started in 1849, everything changed. Trails crisscrossed everywhere. Mule trains, ox-team carts and stage lines developed the roads and trails into Calaveras County. Packers carrying miners' from Angels Camp to Sonora and visa versa traversed the old "Slum-gullion Road" by way of Robinsons Ferry and Tuttletown.

Within four years Wells Fargo ran daily stages from Columbia to Oakdale, Stockton and beyond. This daily service grew to four daily stages, but with the advent of the discovery of richer ores in other regions this all changed. New gold and silver strikes on the Comstock and in Bodie attracted hordes of miners from the Mother Lode. Passenger and freight service into Angels Camp and elsewhere would be cut drastically. Early routes into the

A stage gets underway from Valley Springs headed for Fourth Crossing, Altaville and Angels Camp.

Stage ready to depart from the Commercial Hotel in Angels Camp, to meet the train in Milton.

county came from Stockton via Valley Springs and Fourth Crossing to Altaville, and via the Stanislaus' north shore via Copperopolis to Altaville.

The first trans-Sierra emigrant *trail* through Ebbetts Pass was opened in the early 1850's. In 1861, Calaveras County was one of three Mother Lode Counties that joined together to construct a trans-Sierra *road* over the major route from Sonora to Bridgeport. It was called the Mono road, and was a toll road. Eventually one stage company provided daily service, sometimes taking three weeks for the trip. Another toll road, the "Carson Valley and Big Tree Road", was opened in 1864 through Ebbetts Pass.

TRAINS in the American West would not become much of a reality until after the Central Pacific and the Union Pacific Railroads joined in Promentory Point, Utah, in 1869. This event linked the central and eastern parts of America with Sacramento. The network of railroads fanning out from Sacramento in all directions would be built faster than anyone would imagine. During this period the mines of Calaveras County had changed from surface mines to quartz vein underground mines. Each year they became more productive until a full-fledged industry developed. At the same time lumber interests were growing. The forests had a super-abundance of trees, and soon a full-fledged second industry was developing. Transportation at that time was crude at best. Then along came an Eastern gentleman by the name of Thomas S. Bullock, who was looking to build a railroad somewhere with equipment and rail he owned from his defunct Arizona railroad. He had heard that transportation at the southern mines of California was all animal-led, which was contributing to costly outmoded methods. He set out to gather investors to build a railroad into the Southern mines of Calaveras and Tuolumne Counties.

He made the acquaintance of Prince Andre Poniatowski, a local Calaveras businessman who was busily involved in the development of hydroelectric generation in the area. Poniatowski was well known, well connected, and had numerous financial contacts. His wife was also the sister-in-law of William H. Crocker, wealthy San Francisco banker. Bullock and Poniatowski (see Note below) joined forces in this rail venture, and were able to bring Crocker into the project to provide the required financial backing. In 1897 the original articles of the Sierra Railroad were drawn up and incorporated.

Note: Prince Andre Poniatowski was of Polish noble decent, born in Paris in 1864, came to the United States in 1892, and married Elizabeth Sperry two years later. She was the daughter of a well-known Stockton miller, and niece of James Sperry, prominent hotel proprietor and Big Trees promoter.

The actual route of the Sierra Railroad had not been definitely established at that point. Whether it would go directly into the Calaveras mines or the Tuolumne mines remained to be determined. Poniatowski and Bullock set out by horseback to survey the entire mine area of the two-counties. The previously proposed routes that Bullock had discussed were: 1) An extension of the narrow-gauge San Joaquin and Sierra Nevada Railroad built by a Mr. F. Birdsall in 1885, running from Brack's Landing near Lodi to Valley Springs, but later taken over by the Southern Pacific

A passenger car of the narrow gauge San Joaquin and Sierra Nevada Railroad, running between Lodi and Valley Springs. It was named after the wife of the company's president.

Railroad, and, 2) An altogether new route to the mines of Calaveras County at Angels Camp or to the mines of Tuolumne County. Their horseback ride proved fruitful, because both men decided that the route should originate in Oakdale, and that the first segment of track would be a modest roadbed to Jamestown in Tuolumne County. The railroad construction started March 2, 1897

STOCKTON AND COPPEROPOLIS RAILROAD.

Pass'ger.	Pass'ger.	Mls	*February* 7, 1881.	Mls	Pass'ger.	Pass'ger.
+5 00 P.M.	+7 30 A.M.	0	lve.+ Stockton. ♦ arr.	34	12 15 NO'N	
5 15 "	7 45 "	1	...C. P. R. R. Depot...	33½	12 00 NO'N	9 20 A.M.
5 37 "	8 07 "	6	......Charleston......	28	11 40 A.M.	9 00 "
5 46 "	8 15 "	9	......Walthall......	25	11 33 "	8 54 "
5 54 "	8 23 "	11	........Holden........	23	11 25 "	8 45 "
6 16 P.M.	8 35 A.M.	15	.........Peters'.........	19	11 15 A.M.	8 35 A.M.
	8 58 A.M.	22	lve....Waverly...arr.	8	10 50 A.M.	
	9 20 A.M.	30	arr.....Milton..♦lve.	0	+10 30 A.M.	
6 46 P.M.		20	.....Farmington.....♦	14		8 15 A.M.
7 02 "		23	... .Trigo..........	11		7 54 "
7 22 "		28	..........Clyde........	6		7 36 "
7 50 P.M.		34	arr.. Oak Dale.♦lve.	0		+7 10 A M.

An 1881 passenger schedule of the Stockton & Copperopolis RR.

Locomotive "Copperopolis" and caboose of the Stockton and Copperopolis Railroad, readying departure from Milton.

The first locomotive, an 0-4-0 numbered No. 1, was put to work just as soon as enough track was built. Then in May an eight-year old 0-6-0 locomotive was obtained from the Montana Union Pacific. When the tracks reached Cooperstown in June 1897, the railroad published its first passenger train schedule. It read "Westbound: - Leave Cooperstown 12:30 p.m., Arrive Oakdale, 1:30 p.m. Eastbound: - Leave San Francisco 9:00 a.m. Leave Oakdale 2:30 p.m. Arrive Cooperstown 3:34 p.m." To carry these passengers the railroad brought on a third locomotive, a 4-6-0 Rogers, plus one coach and a mail and baggage car under lease from the Southern Pacific Railroad. Construction of the line from Cooperstown eastward became more and more difficult with each mile, where some grades reached as much as 3% (this percentage represents a rise of three feet for each one-hundred feet of rail). The railroad proceeded through Don Pedro, Dry Creek Canyon, Chinese Station, and reached Jamestown where the first passenger train arrived on November 8, 1897. The fabulous sixty-room Nevills Hotel, located adjacent to the Jamestown depot, was nearing completion at that time.

A 1930's passenger
Timetable for the
Southern Pacific Railroad
Train from Lodi to
Valley Springs.

LODI AND VALLEY SPRING.

172	M	June 15, 1930.	173	....
A M	..	LEAVE] [ARRIVE	A M	....
11 55	0	+.....Lodi.....ठ	9 30	....
12 80	7	....Lockeford..ठ	8 50	....
12 55	11	.....Clements...ठ	8 25	....
1 15	17	......Wallace......	8 03	....
1 55	27	..Valley Springठ	†7 30	....
P M	..	ARRIVE] [LEAVE	A M	....

The extension of the railroad from Jamestown was expected to turn northward via Rawhide Valley and Tuttletown, and onward to Angels Camp. However, a new and very serious threat to the very existence of the railroad itself was manifesting. Other promoters from the Stockton area were actively acquiring financing and right-of-way for a competing railroad to be built from Stockton via Copperopolis and Columbia to Sonora. However, Prince Poniatowski owned a marble mine in Columbia, and Henry Crocker had lumber interests above Sonora. This shifted the focus of the Sierra Railroad toward Sonora to head off this potential competition. In the meantime, the other new railroad venture started laying track toward Copperopolis. All of a sudden they ran out of money, and couldn't pay their tracklayers. Those tracklayers were immediately hired away by the Sierra Railroad.

By the turn-of-the-century, trains were arriving in Tuolumne City (February 1, 1900), and interest was increasing to extend the Tuttletown branch to the Stanislaus River. The railroad's blueprints for that extension required that a fifty-foot high trestle be built, which tempered the interest a bit. Tuttletown was a beehive up to that time. Two major roads crossed there: 1) A north-south road from Angels Camp via Robinsons Ferry to the Big Oak Flat Road, and, 2) An east-west road from Columbia via Reynolds Ferry to Milton and Stockton. The branch line to Tuttletown had already been serving a half-dozen major mines up to that point, and when extended toward the Stanislaus River would serve at least another half-dozen on Jackass Hill. Many small communities were served by the trading posts in Tuttletown. Construction activity on the Angels Camp branch resumed in March of 1901.

On September 10, 1902, with over three thousand cheering citizens, brass bands playing, and fireworks filling the sky, train #10 pulled into town with bunting flying, smoke everywhere, and whistles blowing in tribute to this historical event. This was the first scheduled train arrival in Angels Camp, and was loaded with railroad "brass" and special guests. The celebration went on all day with speeches, and a reception at Dollings Hall. The people of Angels Camp and other communities in the county were thrilled with the prospect of the railroad.

Almost immediately, special excursion trains were promoted, many with sold-out reservations. Baseball excursions, picnic specials, and trains to almost every special event in Jamestown, Sonora, Tuolumne City, and Oakdale were run, many over-sold. Fares for most excursions were always a bargain. A

(Above) With a full head of steam, the "Gus Special" crosses the Stanislaus River bridge. (Below): The early-morning train waits departure from Angels railroad station headed to Jamestown.

special rate of $2.00 per person for a round trip from Oakdale to Angels Camp was charged. It was so popular the railroad had to retrofit some flatcars with seats and railings to accommodate the demand. The regular fare from Angels Camp to Jamestown was $1.50, departing at 6:45 a.m. and arriving at Jamestown at 8:30 a.m. The return trip left Jamestown at 4:40 p.m., arriving in Angels Camp at 6:35 p.m. This less-than-two-hour trip was a vast improvement over the horse and buggy time for the same trip.

Freight became the backbone of the Sierra Railroad. Angels Camp's mines required not only machinery, but an enormous amount of lumber and general merchandise. The logging and lumber industry had become a big part of the county's economy. Freight rates from Angels Camp to Oakdale were $4.50 per ton for carload lots, and $6.50 for lcl. With the publication of these railroad rates, freight teamsters lowered their rate to $5.00 per ton between Angels Camp and Milton. Milton was the terminous of the Stockton and Copperopolis Railroad, and was leased to, and operated by the Central Pacific Railroad. This line was an extension of the Oakdale line, and ran from Stockton, via Charleston, Walthall, Holden, Peters', and Waverly to Milton. Almost everybody thought that the teamsters couldn't hold that rate and still make a profit. They were proven right. Within two months the teamsters had discontinued service to and from Milton. Also, the Central Pacific Railroad's service on the branch line from Stockton to Milton was discontinued, leaving Angels Camp entirely reliant on the Sierra Railroad to carry its freight.

Trains in and out of Angels Camp became very successful. Passenger trains ran with regularity, and freight trains ran as often as required, sometimes two and three trains a day. The Sierra Railroad as a whole was booming. Besides its passenger and excursion business, along with a very successful freight operation, the railroad enjoyed an enormous amount of revenue from special projects such as the building of Pine Crest dam, Melones dam, the extensions of rail service toward Yosemite, and others. Then, in1929 the stock market crash brought everything "to a slow halt".

Freight and passenger revenue was reduced substantially. Then, along came better roads, paved roads, better trucks, better automobiles, all contributing to making it very hard for the railroad to make ends meet. Finally, the bondholders placed the railroad into receivership under the direction of Mr. C. H. Segerstrom, Sr. Management for the new regime fell to Mr. J. E. Taylor. Then, in 1937, the railroad was sold and reorganized into the Sierra Railroad Company, with D. J. Murphy becoming President, and J. E. Taylor retained as manager. The following year the California Railroad Commission granted the railroad permission to discontinue all passenger service. Finally, in March, 1939, the branch line was completely closed, and "Gus's Special" made its last run from Angels Camp. Just a few people came out to the Sierra station up on Depot Road to say good-bye to the trains they had grown to love over the previous 37 years. There wasn't even a coach for that last train, for Old No. 30 was pulling just two flatcars used to carry the rails back to Jamestown. It was on the 12th day of that month that the last main-line passenger train left Tuolumne and pulled into Oakdale to an empty depot and no trains on which to transfer. Both the Santa Fe and Southern Pacific had already discontinued passenger service into Oakdale that same day.

Some of the Angels Camp facilities remain at the end of the millennium, some 61 years after discontinuance. The depot still stands, although now a residence. Parts of the turntable still exist, and a couple of sheds still stand. The sheds of the Manual Lumber Company still stand, next to the rail yard. And perhaps the best of all, we can still see the little wooden passenger coaches that were built especially for the Angels Camp branch, still seen on film and video, shown in movie "Westerns" made for TV and theaters.

The Sierra Railroad today is a different type of railroad. It serves (mainly) three purposes. 1. It services the owners of the lumber mill in Standard, California, transporting lumber and sawdust to market. 2. It operates a "dinner train", with regular departures from Oakdale eastward and back. 3. It serves as the base for an operating arm of the Calif. State Railroad Museum.

A mid-day shot of the Angels empty railroad yard and station, with the turntable and sheds in the background.

CALAVERAS BUSES

Buses arrived on the Calaveras scene in 1914, thanks to a forward-looking venture by a gentleman by the name of Turner Lillie. Prior to the purchase of his first automobile, Lillie hauled freight and passengers by horse-drawn wagons throughout the county. He knew the business, and knew its potential. It was reported in *The Calaveras Prospect* on May 9, 1914, that he had purchased a "New Ford" for service on the new motorized stage route to Stockton.

The family and business was based in Valley Springs prior to the expansion. With roads becoming more reliable each year, highway transport had become a more viable method of transportation. The railroad into Angels Camp had been operating for more than eleven years, with much freight success. However, it was way out of the way for passengers and mail headed to and from Stockton, to travel via Jamestown and Oakdale. Since the hub of transportation in Calaveras County was in Angels Camp, the Lillies packed up and moved there from Valley Springs. Also, much of the mining, logging and supporting industries were centralized in Angels Camp.

Turner Lillie's Calaveras Transit operated its bus service from Angels Camp to Stockton's main terminal on Hunter Square. Business was so good that he ordered two new Packard buses in 1917. However, those two new buses were destroyed by fire at the Stockton dealership. It would take two more years to get delivery on the two new buses, this time "Fageol Safety Coaches". They looked sleek. By 1920 the railroad had lost its prominence as a passenger carrier, and was allowed to cease its service in 1928. Competition for the bus passenger, package delivery and mail contracts became fierce, but Lillie faced it by expanding service, providing better service and by going heavily into debt. His perseverance paid off, and he became more successful each month. On top of it all he also became a Ford dealer in Angels Camp and rented the Stickle Building for both businesses. In 1926, he bought the building.

The regular route from Angels Camp to Stockton was via Altaville, San Andreas, Valley Springs and Linden. Lillie was also allowed to operate a passenger service through Copperopolis, Milton and Farmington to Stockton. This route did not produce very many passengers, but was far superior for hauling mail. A.B. "Dufo" Gualdoni recalls those days vividly, since he was the driver of that run in a Model A Ford two-door sedan or station wagon. He also remembers that one "class" of passenger from the Banana Ranch became steady customers on their way to Stockton for their regular checkup.

Daily runs from Angels Camp to Douglas Flat, Vallecito, Murphys, Brice Station, Avery, Arnold, Dorrington and Camp Connell were always busy. These feeder runs also went as far as

Big Trees State Park and the lodge at Lake Alpine until the snow closed the highway each winter. Frequent runs were also made to Carson Hill and Melones.

Being a major businessman in town, Turner Lillie was summoned to a meeting to deal with the problems of a gas war. The problems weren't solved, but the outcome of this meeting produced the "Angels Boosters", of which Turner was a charter member. It didn't take long for the Boosters to come up with the idea of a frog jump celebration. The club has endured to this day, and the frog jump has become an important part of the annual county fair. Lillie died on January 15, 1935. He was only 65, but had lived a hard and very successful life. His son, Wilbur, and Wilbur's wife Arlene would take over the business, acquiring two new buses in 1936. They, too, were very successful.

Bob Burrowes Photo

Lillie's Calaveras Transit Ford bus in front of the Angels Camp Terminal on Main Street.

Calaveras Transit was sold in 1941 to J. V. "John" Fuzeré. He had the misfortune of operating a bus system during World War II. Gas and tire rationing made things difficult, but John ran the two-bus operation very successfully. He drove one bus and his son Bob ran the second. After the war their daily run to Arnold continued, and on busy days, both buses made the run to Stockton. John operated Calaveras Transit for almost twenty years, selling to his son-in-law G. L. "Swede" Freed. He, along with his wife Dodie, continued a successful operation for another eighteen years, but as the highways continued to become better and faster, passenger volume decreased. Swede had a huge package business, and operated various stretch limousines during his ownership. He retired in 1979.

The operation had become a family-run bus line over those last years. "Swede's" daughter, Lolly, stepped in and managed the company for over four years. She and Cheryl Mossinger, a long-time associate driver, did the driving. Then in 1985 Swede and Dodie sold the business to Art McCurry, whom they knew well. Art was the manager of the Trailways depot in Stockton, the terminal then used by Calaveras Transit in Stockton. Art struggled with the operation for over a year, but was unable to make a go of it. The Freed's had to take the company back, but it became more and more obvious that it couldn't be revived. Calaveras Transit ceased its operation in 1987, having served Angels Camp and the county well for over 75 years.

Public transportation between Angels Camp and Stockton is no longer available. A new bus service was instituted in 1981 by the Calaveras County Human Resources Council, dubbed the "Stage Coach". Its primary transportation was designed for the senior citizen, and was primarily federally funded. Then, in 1999 an entirely new expanded service was inaugurated under the name of "Calaveras County Transit", also heavily federally funded. The Laidlaw company operates this service, under the management of Calaveras County office of COG. Three fixed routes are operated, plus special services for senior nutrition and dial-a-ride trips.

Chapter Seven

BRET HARTE
and MARK TWAIN

This chapter concerns itself with just two individuals. They really don't need any introduction. Angels Camp's two schools, an elementary/middle school and a high school, are named after these prolific men. They achieved credentials during their life that are the envy of all aspiring writers. The legacy they left in this small village is felt daily by many. We present:

FRANCIS BRET HARTE arrived in San Francisco on March 26, 1854, a wild and turbulent place at that time. He and his sister sailed in the Golden Gate aboard the *S.S. Brother Johathan*, a paddle-wheeled steamship from Nicaragua. He had just crossed the isthmus and was only seventeen years old. Frank, as he was known then, was slight of build, with black curly hair and the beginnings of a youthful mustache.

He was a prolific reader in his youth. By age six he had read Shakespeare, then Dickens and a half-dozen other well-known

Bret Harte, as editor of the Overland Monthly

authors of the day. His father died when he was just nine. Elizabeth Harte and her children then settled in New York. At eleven he authored a poem titled "Autumn Musings," which was printed in the *Sunday Morning Atlas.* Late in 1853, Bret's mother married a Colonel Williams and they made their home in Oakland, California. Bret and Margaret were to follow.

The two children sailed from New York on February 20, 1854 on the steamship *Star of the West,* arriving at Greytown, Nicaragua. Their trip across the isthmus was uneventful, arriving in San Juan del Sur via mule and wagon. Their last leg aboard the *S.S. Brother Johathan* was a bit more turbulent. Weather caused major delays, and engine difficulties put one of the two paddlewheels out of commission. They limped into San Francisco eighteen days later.

Harte grew weary after his arrival. Late in '54 he left the home he had made with his mother and new stepfather, even though he had no ill feeling toward Colonel Williams. He was determined to try his hand at anything, so he set out for the California foothills. For the next twelve months Bret worked as a printer, journalist, teacher, miner, and anything else that came along. His first stint was as a teacher in La Grange, but that didn't last long due to lack of students. Bret thought he might try his hand at mining, so he headed due north from La Grange for Robinsons Ferry on the Stanislaus River.

The trek was 40 miles, and he did it by foot. In no time at all he was befriended by two miners who thought it would bring good luck if they teamed up with a novice. The three of them went to work immediately, and Bret found "color" (miner's term for gold) in his first pan of gravel. The three men worked together for three weeks, then moved on to other claims along the Stanislaus. During this wandering, Bret most likely ventured as far as Angels Camp on the north, and Table Mountain on the south, but there is no actual record of those treks. Some of his writings described a countryside that probably was Angels Camp and its surrounding area.

A Pliocene skull was found near Angels Camp in a mine about 150 feet deep. This famous skull became the subject of a poem made famous by Harte, entitled "Society Upon The Stanislow", which goes as follows:

"I reside at Table Mountain, and my name is Truthful James;
I am not up to small deceit, or any sinful games;
And I'll tell in simple language what I know about the row
That broke up our society upon the Stanislow.

"But first I would remark that it is not a proper plan
For any scientific gent to whale his fellow man,
And if a member don't agree with his peculiar whim,
To lay for that same member for to 'put a head' on him.

""Now, nothing could be finer or more beautiful to see
Than the first six months' proceedings of that same society,
Till Brown of Calaveras brought a lot of fossil bones
That he found within a tunnel near the tenement of Jones.

"Then Brown he read a paper and reconstructed there
From those same bones an animal that was extremely rare'
And Jones then asked the chair for a suspension of the rules
Till he could prove that those same bones were one of his lost mules.

"Then Brown he smiled a bitter smile and said he was at fault'
It seemed he had been trespassing on Jones' family vault.
He was a most sarcastic man, this quiet Mr. Brown,
And on several occasions he had cleaned out the town.

"Now, I hold it is not decent for a scientific gent
To say another is an ass-at least, to all intent;
Nor should the individual who happens to be meant
Reply by heaving rocks at him to any great extent.

"Then Abner Dean, of Angel's, raised a point of order, when
A chunk of old red sandstone took him in the abdomen,
And he smiled a kind of sickly smile, and curl'd up on the floor,
And the subsequent proceedings interested him no more.

"For, in less time than I write it, every member did engage
On a warfare with the remnants of a palaeozoic age;
And the way they heaved those fossils in their anger was a sin,
Till the skull of an old mammoth caved the head of Thompson in."

The Gillis brothers had settled on Jackass Hill while working a claim, just a mile south of Robinsons Ferry. Bret became friends with them on a previous occasion. Several months after his mining and wanderings along the Stanislaus River area, Harte decided to head back out of the hills. He hiked toward the Gillis brothers' cabin on Jackass Hill, on his way to San Francisco. He was broke, but determined to return to a place that was more friendly to his way of life. Jim Gillis paid his stage fare and sent him on his way. Harte never returned to this area.

After moving on to live with his mother and stepfather, he obtained a job in a pharmacy, then became a tutor, and finally set out for far northern California to follow his love of journalism. This is were his sister and her husband had settled. He served as an apprentice on a Humboldt County publication, and within a year had become an associate editor. After another year he had a disastrous editorial encounter with an Indian episode that caused his sudden departure for San Francisco.

Bret Harte's *The Luck of Roaring Camp* and *The Outcasts of Poker Flat* are the two of his most famous and enduring stories. He was a prolific writer of wild myths of the American West. He is noted for creating a unique American art form, having written in a multitude of pulp magazines and dime novels. Harte is credited with writing a style of the American frontier that has become the prototype of the "western" movie. His reputation abroad soared, while his reputation on his homeland soured. He spent most of his last years in Europe where he was more honored than on his native land.

At age 42, Bret was appointed United States consul in Crefeld, Germany, and two years later received an appointment as the consul in Glasgow, Scotland. After five years the tenure of his office in Glasgow expired, and he moved to London to devote his entire time to literary work. Bret died in Aldershot, England, at age 65.

SAMUEL LONGHORN CLEMENS was born in Florida, Missouri, on November 30, 1835. His parents were from aristocratic stock, but lacked any great wealth themselves. Sam's experiences as a youth in Hannibal, Missouri, and along the Mississippi would bring us all great pleasure when he later wrote of those events. His older brother, Orion, would prove to be a great influence on his life and times and whereabouts.

Sam had a busy youth. His father passed away when Sam was only 12 years old. He had to go to work to help make ends meet. He started as an apprentice printer, and for the next 10 years supported himself at that trade. He traveled throughout the east in cities such as New York, Philadelphia, St. Louis and Cincinnati, working as a journeyman printer. On a trip from Cincinnati to New Orleans, he apprenticed himself to Horace Bixby as a river pilot. Sam's experiences on the river would later prove to be a major influence on his career as a writer. He amused himself during those days by putting on skits for friends, without thought of professional authorship.

When Sam was in his mid-twenties, he grew impatient with the goings on of the war between the states, and set out to visit his brother in Keokuk, Iowa. The timing was perfect, for, upon his arrival, he was told of a fabulous offer Orion had received to become the secretary to the governor of the Nevada Territory. Lacking the necessary funds to make the trip, Orion was offered the fare for the trip west by Sam if Sam could join him. Sam had hoped to spend just a few weeks out in the Wild West. Orion accepted and the two set out for St. Joseph, Missouri, where they would catch the stage west. The fare was $150 each. After a tumultuous journey of twenty days they arrived in Carson City. Sam loved every minute of the trip. It was just the adventure he wanted.

The two brothers settled in at Carson City. Orion became a very popular man due to his honesty and trustworthiness among the politicians. Sam didn't have any set plans, and chose to explore the

Mark Twain at sixty-five, photograph taken in 1901.

territory around the capitol city. His experiences and dreams in Aurora, Nevada, as a laborer and speculator were short lived. He had, from time to time, sent some travel letters and experiences to the Keokuk *Gate City* and the Virginia City *Territorial Enterprise*, using the nom de plume of *Josh.* They were very well received by the papers' readers, much to the joy of Sam. Much in need of money, he thought that perhaps he'd be able to sell his stories to other newspapers and magazines, so he first offered his letters to the Sacramento *Union*, for $10 a week. About that same time the *Enterprise* would offer Sam a position on the paper's staff. It was there that Sam took the pen name of *Mark Twain.* He became a huge success with the Virginia City newspaper. His associates included such truly great names as William Wright, known as *Dan de Quille,* and John Phoenix, Squibob, and Artemus Ward.

The time had come to move on from Virginia City, so Twain and Steve Gillis boarded the stage for San Francisco. It was May, 1864, and both men joined the staff of the *Morning Call,* Mark Twain as a reporter and Steve Gillis as a compositor. It was here that Mark became acquainted with Bret Harte. They both wound up working in the same building. Harte worked in the U.S. Mint annex on the third floor, and Twain downstairs in the *Morning Call* headquarters. Mark liked Bret Harte immensely. He not only had great respect for his literary prowess, but took great pleasure in his company. The feeling of Bret for Mark was mutual. This deteriorated over the years to a point where the exact reverse finally became a reality.

Mark Twain eventually lost his job on the *Morning Call,* and of course, lost his weekly paycheck. He had several lesser obligations from the *Enterprise* and as a drama reviewer that brought barely enough to keep him from poverty. Meanwhile, his companion, Steve Gillis, got into a barroom brawl and landed in jail. After posting bail Steve decided to jump his bail, head back to Virginia City, and resume his position on the *Territorial Enterprise.* Twain's love of San Francisco was wearing thin. At the same time, Steve's brother Jim Gillis was visiting in San Francisco, so Jim offered his hospitality to Mark to come up to Jackass Hill for the winter. Mark accepted.

This was not Twain's first visit to Jackass Hill or its surroundings. He had been here before for just a short time, and knew the hustle and bustle of the mining towns nearby. This time he was surprised to see some of the ghostly ruins of Angels Camp. He had always remembered the town as a serene paradise. But the mood of the town suited him perfectly, as described in his *Roughing It*. Mark shared the Jackass Hill cabin with not only Jim Gillis, but also Jim's younger brother Billy and a miner named Dick Stoker. The idea of mining for gold and its potential for instant wealth fascinated Mark, but he never seemed to want to actually participate in it. Rather, he preferred to write, often reading his latest opuses to his roommates. They loved it, and took every advantage of teasing and ribbing him.

When Twain was in San Francisco he was used to dining in the opulent and luxurious restaurants, eating scalloped oysters and drinking champagne. But here, he noted in his journal, "January 23, 1865, - Angels – Rainy, stormy – Beans & dishwater for breakfast at the Frenchman's; dishwater and beans for dinner, and both articles warmed over for supper." He went on to note, "30th Jan. Moved to new hotel, just opened – good fare, & coffee that a Christian may drink without jeopardizing his eternal soul." Twain was bored with the small populous of Angels Camp, reminding him of his hometown friends and acquaints. But he took pleasure practicing his French with the proprietor of the café, and when bored would often gather up either Jim or Stoker and head for Angels Camp's Tryon Tavern, a part of the Angels Hotel. They'd all take turns spinning yarns, even Ben Coons, the handsome bartender. One afternoon Ben began a tale about a well-trained frog that would jump on command, but when put up against another frog, the other frog's owner secretly loaded the first frog with buckshot and won the contest. Mark jotted down a few notes of this tale, not because he hadn't heard the tale before, but Ben Coon's style had intrigued him. It, of course, was the basis for

Mark's fabulous story of *The Celebrated Jumping Frog of Calaveras County.*

Twain described other experiences he had in the Stanislaus area. His visit to Vallecito (seven miles east of Angels Camp) prompted an item in his notes reminding him that he had seen a "magnificent lunar rainbow" glowing through a light, misty rain. He had amassed copious notes during his visit with Jim Gillis, yet little did he know what vast yarns would come of this two-month visit. He left on February 24, 1865, for San Francisco, by way of Copperopolis, returning to the cosmopolitan life he loved so much.

Chapter Eight

PEOPLE AND PLACES

Pioneers and their Families

The first families of Angels Camp were indeed pioneers in every sense. Without police or fire protection, and certainly without many of the basic necessities of life, these citizens struggled every minute of the day just to get things done. On the other hand, there were doctors, plenty of transportation (horses, wagons, buggies, buckboards, stages, etc.), adequate supplies of food, basic schools, and good entertainment (of the day). Here are a few of the outstanding leaders and pioneers of Angels Camp, not in any particular order:

Henry P. Angel, along with his brother George, founded Angels Camp in 1848. The brothers were born in Rhode Island, and came to California as soldiers serving under Fremont during the Mexican War. Pitifully little has been written about the Angel brothers. It has been reported that Henry was in Sutter's Fort in February 1848. He was next reported at Monterey in May of that year, where

Henry P. Angel

both brothers joined the 92-man Carson-Robinson expedition to the goldfields. In September it was reported that Henry Angel was camped, and was placer mining at the confluence of Dry Creek and Angels Creek. Others in the party mined further south, and on what came to be known as Carson Creek – in the Carson Hill area.

In October or November Henry gave up mining due to weakness caused by a previous bout with Malaria during the war. He opened his trading post at a time when fewer than 300 miners dotted the countryside. George joined him in the venture almost immediately. T. H. Hittell, a California historian at that time, reported that their store was in operation in mid-December, 1848. Their operation of the post was short-lived, for they sold out to J. C. Scribner in 1849. George Angel seemed to drop from the local scene, and probably moved on to Oregon, or returned to the East.

Henry, too, seemed to drop from the picture for five years. Then, in 1854, a newspaper reported that he had completed building the "commodious" Cave House Hotel at Cave City. During the next years, Henry worked as a gravel mine owner, and lived in Calaveritas and Fourth Crossing. He followed his life-long friend and business partner, Henry Odell, in death at the County Hospital in San Andreas, on March 17, 1897. His obituary stated that "Mr. Angel was highly respected by all who knew him and had not a known enemy in the world."

Alexander Love, a native of Edinburgh, Scotland, arrived in 1851 with his wife Jane, and daughter Elizabeth, who went to the town's first school at the corner of Main Street and Rasberry, where the Veterans Building now stands. He took out homestead papers on a sizeable piece of property on Main Street, then known as "Stage Road in the village of Angels". He built his home, a dairy, a lumber mill (on Love Creek near Avery), and served as County Assessor for twelve years. Love's home was on Bush Street, next to Benager Rasberry, who was not only a neighbor, but a good friend. Love's property holdings also included a plumbing shop and Angels Camp's first movie theatre. The family kids used to climb into a loft of the plumbing shop and sneak a free peek of the movie or show. They also delivered milk to the dairy's customers. The dairy was converted later into a livery stable. He started with just one horse and buggy, but the business thrived to the point where he had almost 30 horses, buggies, surreys carriages carts, and lumber wagons. The Pioneer Stable was later turned into a garage, and given a new slab concrete floor. The garage was torn down in March of '71, but the slab floor still sits silently awaiting a future.

Love gave each of his grandchildren a lot on the homestead where they all built their homes. Daughter Elizabeth, married a Lewis McGaffey, from Lyndon Center, Vermont. They had four children. Lewis died very young, when their daughter Jennie was only eleven years old. "Grandma" McGaffey (Elizabeth) was a "real mother", says granddaughter Rose Fletcher. She was always home, and the family always gathered around her. If someone was sick she was always there. The family's holiday activity centered at Grandma's house.

The McGaffey's daughter, Jennie, married Henry Hogarth, who was a mill man, and loved mining. They had five children, Alvin, Harry, Ruth, Rose and Bessie. All five attended the elementary school on Finnegan Lane. Rose married John Fletcher, the son of Otto Fletcher and Martha Rasberry. John worked in the mines and served a 20-year career with PG&E. John and Rose begat two sons, Jack and Donald. Jack was killed during WWII while Don also served in WWII and went on to become one of the area's leading contractors, and served on Angels Camp's Planning Commission. Don, with his wife Faye, had two children, Janice & Jack. Jack continues the legacy of Fletcher Construction. He and his wife are the proud parents of Jessica and Alexandria.

Ruth Hogarth served as "telephone central", located in the Drug Store. She married Charlie "Chappo" Eberhardt. They had two children, Marion and Wilbur. Wilbur served in WWII in the merchant marine, and then joined his father as the distributor in

Angels Camp for Standard Oil Company. He and his wife Arlene had two children, Ronald and Paul. Ron's career has been with Angels Food Market. He has one son, Anthony. Paul's children are David and Ronald,.

John Pierano was a native of Genoa, Italy. Born in 1824, he set out by sailing vessel at age 25 by way of the Isthmus of Panama, and arrived in San Francisco about 1850. He had hoped to make a fortune in the California goldfields, and help his folks back home. He was a smallish man, fair-skinned with blue eyes, and had red hair and beard. He always wore a smile.

Upon arrival in Angels Camp in 1850, John pitched his tent on Angels Creek, immediately jumped into mining, and became a success within just two years. Wisely, he purchased a large piece of property on the south side of the creek, built his home and a pond with ditch to the creek. This supplied water to his new vineyard and orchard. Still unmarried, John took a fancy to Joseph and Nettie Podesta's daughter, Julia. The Podestas, from Baltimore, were innkeepers in Columbia. John and Julia were soon married, and had three children, Joseph (b. 1860), Nettie (b. 1863), and John (b. 1866). Sadly, Johnnie died in childhood.

John opened his first store in a tent in 1853, south creekside on Main Street. The next year he built his stone building just across the creek, on Main Street at Birds Way. John and Julia then built a new two-story home behind the store. Their store became the center of activity for much of the early days. It was a general merchandise store that marketed everything from food to yardage fabric. Their adjoining rock-based residence has walls eighteen inches thick, and is still occupied by a direct decendant, Mrs. Barbara Lemue Richards. Nettie's mother thought that she was too much of a tomboy as a young girl, so Nettie was sent to a finishing school in Benicia. After several years she returned to Angels Camp a vivacious and attractive young lady. She met the love of her life, and married Canadian-born Ralph Lemue. They had one child, John Peirano Lemue, born on September 25, 1891. John, along with his father Ralph, bought the Angels Hotel from Otto Dolling in 1917. John operated the hotel for 29 years. He served in WWI, and while on duty in San Diego, married Ruth Harper. His bride was a direct decendant of another area pioneer, Wade Hampton Johnston. Ruth and John had two children, Barbara Marie (b. 1923) and John Harper (b. 1920). They both still reside in the area, John and wife Betty (Hankammer) Lemue in Vallecito, and Barbara (Lemue) Richards in the family home in Angels Camp. The youngest decendant of the family today is the great-great grandson of pioneer John Peirano, Robert John Lemue, son of John and Betty.

Michael Cosgrove, a native of St. Louis, Missouri, along with his wife Catherine, arrived in San Francisco in March, 1852. She was "with child", and gave birth to Charles James Cosgrove on July 15th of that year. Three weeks later, they moved to Angels Camp. Michael built their home on Main Street, and also embarked on a building venture that would produce a hotel, a livery stable, and a carriage house. The hotel was located on Main Street where the Utica Hotel (originally named the Bazinett Hotel) now stands. Just below, and next door he built his livery stable.

Cosgrove operated the livery stable for a while, but turned the business over to John Ferry, who called it the Angels Stable. The fire of 1885, which started in the upper story of the Cosgrove Hotel, destroyed many buildings on both sides of the street. The stable, along with their hotel burned to the ground. The hotel was rebuilt and sold to Mrs. Slibbets Eddy in 1893. The "Woods Building" was built in the livery stable location.

Charles Cosgrove married Mary E. Bryan in 1878. She was a local girl from San Andreas. They had a daughter and two sons. The two sons were named Burton H. Cosgrove and Elmer L. Cosgrove, and their sister was named Annetta, later Mrs. Earl Chapman. Annetta Cosgrove Chapman was a prolific and very capable historian, and has chronicled her family's history over the years. One child was born to Annetta and Earl Chapman in 1913,

Jeanette. She married Herbert Scott in 1945, and passed away on April 9, 1956.

Michael Cosgrove died in 1868. Seven years later his widow purchased 30 acres from the Matson Estate, and built a home on the parcel which was located between the Gold Cliff Mine and Hardscrabble Street. She lived there for many years, then sold the property to the Utica Mining Company. The flood of 1909 caused the loss of many of the family's artifacts and old relics that were stored in the old carriage house on Angels Creek. Other businesses along the creek suffered major damage. Then in 1913, the family built one of the first garages in the county, and rented it to John Carley. In 1926 the creek flooded again and washed the garage away. Then in 1946 their home was condemned to enable the State to build a bridge across Angels Creek. The garage was rebuilt, and a parking lot was extended next door.

Michael Cosgrave, a native of County Cork, Ireland, came to Calaveras County in 1852. This "Michael" is often confused with the other "Michael Cosgrove" just heretofore mentioned. This "Michael" is spelled with an "A". He and his brother Jeremiah, who never married, were driven out of Ireland by the potato famine. Michael had seven children, all of which chose a different career, with the exception of George and David. These two gentlemen studied the law, David practicing the law, and George becoming a federal judge. Michaels other children were Jim, Jeremiah, Anna, Mary and John, who became a sheriff. David's only child, David E. Cosgrave, married Pearl Guisto, and settled in at the ranch just north of Angels Camp. Their children were Laurie Ann, Diana (Lewis), Angels Camp librarian, and David, a devoted lifelong teacher at Angels Camp's Mark Twain Elementary School.

Olivia Eleria Rolleri was brought into this world in San Antonia de Castiglione, Italy on August 1, 1844. Her papa was Giovanni Filippo Antonini, who came to Sonora, Tuolumne County, in the late 1840's. He left his wife and their two small girls in the hills of the Italian Riviera until he was able to send the funds for them to join him. Olivia promised her girlfriends at home that she would send them necklaces made of gold. Papa sent for his family in the mid-fifties. The girls and their mother came by boat from Genoa, around the Horn, to San Francisco where they were met and taken to Sonora.

One of John Antonini's Italian friends, John Marconi, was promised the hand of Olivia upon her arrival, which was the custom in the old country in those days. Olivia met many young men who greeted them, one being John Marconi. She also met another young Italian, Geronimo Rolleri, who was younger, more dashing, and more persuasive than Marconi. Her independence prevailed, she refused the hand of Marconi (who later won the hand of Olivia's sister, Emanuela), and married Geronimo (some reported spelling: Gerolimo). They established their home in Big Oak Flat, and lived in different parts of Tuolumne County over the next 20 years. They ventured into mining, ranching and store-keeping, sometimes all three. In 1879 they moved to Reynold's Ferry, on the Stanislaus River. The older Rolleri brothers helped in the operation of the ferry. The family did not run a regular hotel, but often cared for an occasional guest. One of their "guests" was Black Bart. In 1883, while still living at Reynold's Ferry, James Rolleri made his famous shot at Black Bart while James was riding "shotgun" near Funk Hill.

Grandma Olivia Rolleri

Geronimo Rolleri died of pneumonia in 1888. Olivia had brought 13 children into this world. Two died in infancy, and daughter Mary married and went to live in Yankee Hill. This left 10 children to care for. Olivia had plenty of courage, but lacked funds. She let it be known that she was looking for a business to run. She received several excellent offers, but had heard of a possibility in Angels Camp that seemed attractive. She investigated and bought the property, the first unit of the Calaveras Hotel. Olivia moved the family, and opened for business.

Over the next few years her success was paying off, and property on both sides of the hotel was becoming available. She acquired both to the left and to the right of the original property, and then expanded the corner building on Main and Hardscrabble Streets. The service and food she offered was so superior that the hotel grew to 54 rooms, the largest in Angels Camp. Deciding to supply the hotel restaurant herself, she purchased some ranches, ran cattle, opened a saloon and butcher shop, and produced milk and butter, chickens, meat, fruit, vegetables and eggs. Her boys worked the ranches, and her girls helped at the hotel. Cooking at

Grandma Rolleri's fabulous & regionally famous Hotel Calaveras

the hotel was done by Chinese chefs, who "Grandma" taught to make delicious Italian dishes. Willie Lee was one of the best ravioli makers in the Mother Lode.

Olivia's hotel, restaurant and saloon, had gained an outstanding reputation. On a Sunday afternoon, townsfolk would line up at the kitchen door with buckets to buy several ladles of her famous raviolis. The food in her restaurant was "the best in the Mother Lode", and the waitresses and saloonkeepers always dressed in the "finest" of the day. The hotel burned to the ground in 1938.

George Clifton Tryon, was born in New York, the youngest of seven sons of John and Eliza Tryon, natives of Dublin and Edinburgh respectively. When only 14, George left home to find work. It wasn't until he was twenty-one that he sailed from New York to Panama, crossed the Isthmus by foot, then sailed north where he encountered what could have been a major tragedy. His boat became shipwrecked, he swam ashore, and traveled the rest of the way by foot, arriving in San Francisco in June of 1849.

In 1850 he came to Mokelumne Hill, mined for several years, then making his move to Angels Camp in 1853. One of his very first jobs was as a cook in the Angels Hotel. Mark Twain's famous remark about "dishwater and beans" came about as a result of his bettering his eating habits by switching to George Tryon's cooking in the Angels Hotel. In '63 Tryon bought the hotel, and successfully operated it for 24 years. George was well known throughout Calaveras County having served two terms as county Assessor, also Assessor of internal revenue and Deputy Sheriff. He ran for Sheriff in 1862 and was elected. In '64 he was reelected for another term.

In 1856 George was married to Adelia Newman. They had eleven children, with four dying in their youth. Only one of their children remained in Angels Camp, their son Charles. Charles was a hard working and respected businessman. He assumed the responsibilities of the family livery stable, and was one of the early promoters of the Jumping Frog Jubilee. He was also active in cattle raising. The family ranch, which is partially within the city limits, was adequate enough to feed Charles' cattle herd in the winter, but toward the end of spring, he took his cattle to Highland Lakes to graze for the summer. He was the first to use this source for grazing in the High Sierra.

Charlie and Catherine Tryon met and were married in their youth. They had no children, but their nephew, Walter, was treated just like their son. When Walter was older he joined Charles in the cattle business, and in 1941 went on to marry Lucy van Loben Sels. Charlie's health deteriorated somewhat, so they sold some of their cattle interests. Walter and Lucy moved to Chicago where their two oldest sons were born, John and Tom. Tom moved back here to the ranch, married Denise Wakefield, started a new herd of cattle, raised a family – Elizabeth, Kate and Walter – and became prominent on his own by successfully representing the Angels Camp district as county supervisor for four terms. He also ran for lieutenant governor of California on the Libertarian ticket in 1998.

George Clifton Tryon and the four generations that have succeeded him have left a legacy in Calaveras County for which they can be proud. The Tryon ranch, which played a part in the development of the railroad, Tryon Meadows and Mt. Tryon in the high Sierra, and the hundreds of ventures that the family touched, all have made the lives of many of our local citizens richer.

Otto Dolling, born in Germany in 1849, was raised in Holstein, and when 20 years old, came to California and located in Knight's Ferry. For the next 16 years he prospected for gold in different localities, became quite successful, finally owning three Calaveras mines, the Claude, Black Oak and Gold Valley. He was also a ranching partner with his brother in Washington State. In 1888 he bought the Angel's Hotel from George C. Tryon, renovated it, and ran "one of the best appointed hotels in the mountains." Comfort and convenience were foremost services in

Dolling's hotel. He also operated Dolling's Hall, a widely used hall in the city. In '86 he married Mary Stickle, daughter of George Stickle (see next Bio).

George Stickle, was born a New Yorker in 1824, the eighth of ten children. His first career was in trunk making, but at

Here are 15 of the most important men in Angels Camp during the 19th century. The occasion of this photo is an Oyster Dinner given by George and Ed Stickle on May 20, 1889. Their guests are: (front row, three seated men, l to r): Thomas "Bud" Miller, George L. Thomas, Dr. J. P. Sylvester. (second row, l to r): D. C. Demarest, Joseph B. Rank, Capt. C. Gibson, Geo. B. Shearer, Thomas Hardy, and Dr. Wm. A. Kelley, with hat, (top row, standing, l to r): Allen Taylor, Geo. C. Tryon, J. C. Scribner, Guin Raymond, Geo. Stickle, and Ed Stickle.

age seventeen, he and his brother left for California. George sailed from San Francisco up the San Joaquin River to Stockton where he went into business for one year. In 1852 he came to Angels Camp and engaged in the mercantile business. Just four years later he erected a stone building, and moved his business into the new location. This building still stands, after surviving several major town fires.

That same year (1856), Stickle ventured into mining. He owned the Stickle Mine before finally selling to F. K. Bechtel of Alameda County, who, in turn, sold the property to the Utica group. The Stickle Mine was one of the most productive of all the mines in Angels Camp, and continued to be for many years. He

Stickle store in the very early 1900's, on downtown Main Street in Angels Camp. Right doorway is George Stickle and his son. On the balcony is Edna Bryan Buckbee, Angels Camp's foremost historian of the twentieth century, along with her sister in the doorway.

married Helen Gillett, and had three children, Mary, George, and Hattie. Mary became the wife of Otto Dolling (see just above). George had, and earned, one of the finest reputations of any man in Angels Camp. His enterprises were always of top repute. He helped organize the first Republican Party in town, served as a school Trustee, and was postmaster for several years.

Robert Leeper, (b. 1836) left home at seventeen years and headed to New Mexico with a drove of cattle. He remained in the cattle business, then came overland to Sacramento by train with 100 head of cattle. His next endeavor was driving a delivery wagon in San Francisco, but almost immediately headed for the mines. He began his mining career in Placer County, and remained in mining for the rest of this lifel.

He married Miss Susan B. Stevens in 1863, and they had two children, Julia and Frank. Leeper acquired the Utica Mine by invoking a process known as claim-jumping, and after a time worked the mine. He built his mansion in 1882, where he and Susan lived for two years. He sold the mansion and his interest in the mine in 1884 to Charlie Lane and his investors for $10,000.

D. D. Demarest is one of the three non-Angels Camp pioneers we wish to highlight. He was proprietor of the Altaville Foundry and Machine Shop, born in New Jersey in 1824. He was the third child of his parents, David S. and Margaret Demarest, who had eleven children. He left school at age eleven and went to work in the field as a plowman. In '42 he learned the trade of blacksmithing, and continued in the trade for seven years. It was then time to move on, so he chose California as his next home. He arrived in San Diego in December, 1949, then sailed north to San Francisco by steamer

With his excellent background in blacksmithing, he went to work in the mining field as a ditch superintendent. In 1861 he bought the property which subsequently housed his famous foundry. Demarest was constantly enlarging and improving his foundry, making castings in not only iron, but also brass, and up to four tons. His blacksmithing and horse-shoeing business gradually grew to a point where he built a new machine shop which did work on a much grander scale. He and Salina Ward were married in '61, and their three children were David, Clarence and Lillie.

Harvey Wood, of Robinson's Ferry, is also a famous pioneer of the area. He was postmaster at Robinson's Ferry, and was always identified with the best of that area. Born in New York State in 1828, Harvey was one of the family of six children whose parents were Alfred and Electa Wood. At 15 Harvey left home, and for the next five years worked as a clerk in New Jersey. In '49, with 53 other young men, left with the Kit Carson Association, and came via Texas overland to Santa Barbara, California. They arrived on the Stanislaus River in July of that year, and Wood settled in Robinsons Ferry where he has lived ever since. After mining for seven years, he bought the ferry which he ran from 1856 to at least 1892. His biography in that year said, "...for twenty years has been agent for the South Carolina mines. He owns the Adelaide mines, which are perhaps the richest in the county." He was also a rancher, and had a well-known beautiful home. Wood was appointed Postmaster at Robinson's Ferry in 1879, and held that position for years. In '64 he married Marinda Gee. Their children were Carlton, Percey and Allie. His bio closed with the comment that, "He is one of the very best and most substantial citizens of Calaveras County."

Charles D. Lane is probably the least well-known of all of these pioneers or leaders, but could arguably be picked as the most important person to step foot in Angels Camp. He was here only 28 years of his life, but they were "some years!" Charley Lane was an experienced miner, and coupled with a little bit of luck, put together a consolidated mine that would be acclaimed around the world. He was the Superintendent (and part owner) of the Utica Consolidated Mining Company.

Lane came from Missouri. His father, Thomas W. Lane, married Janet Tulloch, for whom Tulloch Lake was named. He was only 12 when his mother, father and most of his seven brothers and sisters, departed Missouri and arrived in California's San Joaquin Valley. Their effort at farming was short-lived. Thomas bought a hotel in Knight's Ferry, and owned and operated a Hot Springs Resort in Salt Springs Valley. Charlie didn't seem to be interested in these ventures, since the "glitter" of gold was an attraction he couldn't resist, and the "gold rush" was in full swing.

Charles D. Lane

Charlie went mining. He worked in Calaveras' Alta Mine, also in Amador County's Middle Bar area on the Mokelumne River, then on to Angels Camp where he continued mining and married Anna Garrard, raising a family of five children. He was an ambitious man, always looking for opportunities he could develop. Unable to find that opportunity, he and Anna and the family moved on, where he found work in Battle Mountain, Nevada. Then, they farmed in Southern Idaho where he tried his hand at hydraulic mining. He turned a profit there, but decided to move back to California's Del Norte County where he successfully operated another placer mine. After a while, he became aware that hydraulic mining would soon be outlawed, so he divested his Del Norte interests, and moved back to Angels Camp. He had been gone twelve years.

The Utica Mine, at that time called the Invincible, had been bought and sold, leased and re-leased many times over the previous 20 years. Charles Lane not only knew much of the mine's history, but was optimistic about its potential. He gathered investors together and bought it. It still didn't create much profit for its owners over the next few years. Ownerships changed several times, but Lane kept his optimism, and continued operating the mine. He began adding neighboring mining claims to his operation, finally acquiring the Stickle, Rasberry, Brown, Washington, Confidence,

Egan, Little Nugget and Gold Cliff Mines. He also bought the Union Water Company to insure ample water. The consolidated mine was on its way to riches. The shafts were deepened, the mining crew was expanded, and "luck" was shining its head. It wasn't long before the Utica started showing big profits. In one month it brought in over $600,000. Charlie Lane had become a wealthy man.

Opportunity knocked again for Charlie. In later years, he took his fortune and his wife to Alaska. He put almost everything he had into a new mining venture. It proved to be an ill-fated investment. His mining operation never produced a profit. He became blind, and At age 71, died at the home of

Bennager Rasberry

his daughter in Palo Alto, California on May 26, 1911.

Bennager Rasberry, a successful pioneer, lives in history with a tale that is said to have him cleaning his rifle one day, when his ramrod rammed. Attempting to shoot it from his gun, after missing a squirrel, and struck a manzanita bush. When retrieving his ramrod, he found that it was imbedded in the bush and a piece of gold laden quartz. That afternoon he took out seven hundred dollars worth of gold, the next day two thousand dollars worth, and the next day for seven thousand dollars. He continued working the vein for several months, and became a rich man.

There were literally dozens of pioneers and leaders of Angels Camp. Archie ("Mr. Mother Lode") Stevenot and Barden Stevenot would easily qualify in that category. Others, such as Oliver "Barney" Bernasconi, Clyde Nash, Brad Pecchinino, Dave Copello, Charlie Wistos, Ralph Lemue, Charlie and Frank Crespi, Charlie Monte Verda, Joe and Earl Carley, Carl Whitley, Harry, Glenn and Mike Croshaw, Hank and Bob Middleton, Giacomo Oneto, Jim Valente, Loren Whittle, Tim and Tad Faleldorf, Floyd and Buck Segale, Paul, and Mel Soracco would be classed as major players in Angels Camp's history. Many of these men and women have fathers and grandfathers that were just as reputed. The list goes on, and on, and on. We couldn't possibly include them all, but we surely salute them.

Angels Camp Ranches

These good neighbors of Angels Camp were indeed citizens of the town. Their influence, often enormous, not only included a food supply, but their individual input on committees and commissions was of utmost importance. These family ranches, most of which have endured through many generations, and most still existing today, include the Tryon ranch, several Airola families' ranches, Don Pierano ranch, the Onetos, Canepas, Whittles, Fragueros, Albasios, Osbornes, Cosgraves, Warners, Meachams, Bernasconis, Pontes, and the most well-known ranch of the Spence family.

A rare photo out on the Whittle ranch. This is the first surrey in Angels Camp. The men are (front seat) Bill Beyers and a mine superintendent Mr. Hodges. Don and Harry Whittle are in the back seat. This picture was taken in front of the original family home out on the ranch.

Chapter Nine

POTPOURRI

The *POPULATION* of Angels Camp varied over the years, reflecting the activity of the city, whether it was abuzz with mining, or in a lull when the mines were quiet. The first year that records of the town's population were kept appears to be in 1870. Starting with that year, and each ten years thereafter, the populations were 1,748, 1,381, 1,950, 4,258, 3,370, 2,224, and 1,894 in year 1930. The population in 2000 is 3,062*. Growth during the 1990's has been rapid, due to the development of Greenhorn Creek resort and golf course, the Angels Oaks expansion, and several other major projects in the city.

The 1870 record further indicated that there were 222 Chinese living in the town, but only four blacks and three domesticated Indians (the census didn't count non-domesticated Indians).

The entire population of Calaveras county in 1850 (our first year of statehood) was 16,884, of which 98% were males. Ten years later the population remained almost exactly the same, but only 84% were male, with female growth from 2% to 16%. Then, in 1870 the total county population plummeted to 8,895, but has grown to 38,476 in January, 2000*.

The *SUBURBS* of Angels Camp were numerous. The original city limits consisted of just a few acres. Main Street in the city ended at Angels Creek on the south and the catholic church on the north. Getting around wasn't at all easy. The suburbs of the town each developed a name and core. "Purdyville" was one of the first, along with Democrat Hill, Circus Hill and Altaville. Purdyville was developed mostly by Serbians and Italians, and was located just east of the Serbian church in the area now containing streets such as Bret Harte, Stork, South Baker, Summit, and Purdy Road. The Dead Horse Mine was located here, and the community had numerous boarding houses. Each of these boarding houses served as the local bar, local café, and of course a miner's home and bed. Most made their own wine, and most made their wine from the Mission variety of grape. These enclaves were not located between specific streets or perimeters, but rather were general areas that each person would perceive them to be. At the southeast perimeter of Purdyville laid a hill area called "Circus Hill, the site of the Utica Cross Shaft..

Democrat Hill was developed high on the hill behind what is now the Visitors Center and Parking area. The lower portion of Democrat Hill, along Bush St., Hardscrabble, Love St., etc., was in the city limits. The upper section now has Fairview and Mark Twain as its thoroughfares.

All of the area south of the Angels Creek bridge was not originally in the city. The old timers in the area now call it the "annex", presumably because it was annexed to the city in more recent times. The town's baseball diamond was there, across from today's car wash where Hamm's Storage, Auto Court & Grocery

* - Official county estimate, and official city estimate.

A very early Purdyville neighborhood picture, perhaps 1870's.

Mrs. Kapor's Purdyville boarding house, located on Bret Harte Rd., between Stagg Rd. and Purdy Rd. She was the grandmother of Celia Beltramo. This was the home of mostly Serbian, but also some Italian mineworkers.

complex is located (a mile south of the bridge). This was a very active sports area for Angels Camp. There were also several businesses just south of the Angels Creek bridge, such as the brewery, ice house, hospital, and hotel. There is now an effort afoot to annex more of the area south of the "annex", to the road off of Highway 49 that takes you to the New Melones marina, known by some today as Glory Hole Road, or Whittle Road. Some important developments are planned for that area, including a tri-county fire dispatch center. That district, from Gun Club Drive southward, was called Albany Flat, some say stretching all the way to the Romaggi home. During the early days Albany Flat was a very active mining district, and yielded good fortune for many owners. Today, the area is home to OARS, a statewide white-water rafting organization owned by the George R. Wendt family, and also a new modern parcel facility for UPS. Also located just south of Albany Flat is a boat/household storage business, an RV park, and the Glory Hole store and gas station. More and more people are now referring to the area as the "Glory Hole" area. (this name has been 'borrowed' from the nearby Carson Hill Morgan Mine, affectionately referred to as the Glory Hole).

Another addition or annex to Angels Camp is the town of Altaville in 1972. This was always a suburb, but for most of its existence was thought to be "practically" a part of Angels Camp. Altaville was also called "Forks in the Road" and "Cherokee Flat" in the early period. Today, Angels Camp city limits has moved from St. Patrick's Catholic Church north to Copello Park. Only a post office remains to be identified with the name "Altaville".

Dogtown Road led to (and still leads to) "Dogtown". But don't go looking for Dogtown. It really never existed, and doesn't exist today. Dogtown was just a very scattered community along the 6.7-mile stretch of road on the way to Esmeralda on the San Domingo Creek. It had some of Angels Camp's most celebrated citizens. Some were rich, most lived in cabins, but there were no saloons, no streets, no post office, and no hotels. But, one of the

Angels Camp's ballpark, in the south annex area.

Main Street in Altaville, Prince & Garibardi building on the left.

An early day Dogtown landmark, the DeLarivier House, partly a store, and partly a stopping place for teamsters and travelers.

Angels Brewery, with Joe Raggio holding the horse.

largest homes was a frame building built by the DeLarivier family. Mr. DeLarivier operated a store in his home with a partner, and also provided meals, and had dances and parties. This was the main meeting place for locals, teamsters and travelers. Dogtown also could boast having a blacksmith shop, and a schoolhouse. The school was called The San Domingo School, or sometimes The Dogtown School. Some kids walked four or five miles to get there. Walter Valente recalls, "there used to be 25 or 30 kids, and I graduated out of the eighth grade". The school was operated from 1884 to 1920, and was annexed to Altaville.

Another nearby school, the Washington Flat school, was in session from 1860 until perhaps 1880, with as many as twenty pupils. A decline in mining caused it to close, but in 1896 things changed. The old school building was cleaned and repaired, and started a new life that lasted 34 years. In 1930 the school was closed, and the building was moved to make an addition to the Volf residence. Washington Flat school was located on Murphys Grade Road, just below the French Gulch Road intersection.

The *NEWSPAPERS* of Angels Camp usually didn't last very long. Of the nine papers that were published in the city, only four survived over ten years. Those were the *Monitor*, published from 1879-1889; the *Mountain Echo,* published from 1889-1907; the *Angels Camp Record,* published from 1899-1918; and the longest run for any newspaper in Angels Camp, the *Calaveras Californian,* from 1923 to date. James Nugent was the first publisher. Later Sen. Jesse Mayo became publisher, then Mr. And Mrs. Louis Petithomme, then the Jim Woods, then John Peterson for over 30 years. Just recently sold, the *Californian* is still being published, but today it appears to have been relegated to little more than a "shopper". The earliest newspaper to be published in Angels Camp was the *Calaveras Mountaineer,* but it lasted only one year, 1872-1873. Only four issues of that semi-weekly paper are known to exist. They are all in the Bancroft Library at the University of California in Berkeley.

Probably the first *AUTO DEALER* in the city was Turner Lillie. He became the Ford dealer in about 1924, selling Model T's from his showroom in the Stickle Building. Then, in 1926 John Carley opened a Chevrolet dealership in his garage near Angels Creek. This was a sub-franchise from the Menzies Chevrolet dealership in Stockton. Carley also became a sub-franchiser of the Chalmers and Reo automobiles. Just prior to WWII he also sold Dodges.

Dietz Motors opened their dealership selling Fords, Lincolns and Mercurys, presumably succeeding the Lillie franchise. Up Main Street on the West side in the old Love Dairy-Livery Stable location was Charlie Stone, selling Dodges and Plymouths. Further up Main Street on the other side came the Wilmshurst Chevrolet dealership. That franchise has now changed to a Suburu/Isuzu outlet. Two more dealers opened shop in Angels Camp. In the Bartoo Garage (Mikes Pizza location) was the International truck showroom, and at the north end of town was the Livery Stable, selling Chevrolets, and owned by John Tarter. The Livery Stable closed just a year after it opened. As of this writing, only one has survived. Dick Wilmshurst, with his V.P. and General Manager Alan Corell, has continued to successfully operate their Forty-Niner family dealership for over 46 years.

PHYSICIANS and surgeons served Angels Camp well throughout its history. Those who practiced during the gold rush days were: J. I. Boon, I. C. Isabel, J. C. S. Baker, William A. Kelly, William Jones, L. Lichau, Royal Mills Lampson, George Posey, and I. Sylvester.

As the mining turned to quartz mining, these doctors ministered well: Fred P. Clark, G. Alexander, John R. Dorroh, George Cooper, George F. Pache, R. Raines, Llewlyn Johnston, Charles Freeman, Robie Wendell West, Harry Sevenman, Otis Spaulding, Mabel Gerrard Spaulding, and Elmer Weirich. In the later years, during the post-mining era, these doctors served well:

Ione Dzuber, the Weikles, and Dante Albasio. At the millennium Angels Camp is fortunate to have a very complete consortium of doctors: A. Gerard, J. Bouteller, A. Donaldson, R. Haymond, P. Jacobson, J. Jaggy, E. Lopez, C. Lovett, and S. Nichols.

The Jumping Frog JUBILEE, undoubtedly the biggest celebration of the year, came about as the result of a "gas war" dispute. On April 13, 1925, leaders of Angels Camp called for a meeting "to talk out their problems and work for the betterment of the community." In the final analysis, the most important thing to come out of this meeting was the establishment of the "Angels Boosters", a group whose aim was to "boost" the business conditions of the city. The Boosters immediately came upon the idea of a frog-jumping contest. The very first celebration was a huge success, and was tied in with the celebration of paving downtown's Main Street. The Booster's free swimming pool has also had a long-standing success rate. Many other efforts have proven to have a marked improvement in the affairs of the city.

The "Frog Jump" – as it is affectionately called today – is now integrated into the Calaveras County Fair, held over the third weekend of May at Frogtown (the name given to the fairgounds, three miles south of the city). The contest continues to be run by the Angels Boosters. Participants, or "frog jockeys", have come from every corner of the U.S. and the world.

The DANCE HALLS of Angels Camp were numerous in earlier days. There was dancing, of course, just about anywhere two people could get together, such as bars and night clubs. However, the joy and art of dancing was mainly practiced in the halls built specifically for dancing. Probably the most exciting, active, and popular dance hall of all was Woods Hall. Woods Hall occupied the entire second floor of what was popularly known as the Wells Fargo Building. Operas from the Chattaqua Circuit, high school graduations, and numerous other activities were also held in Woods Hall. This was the social center of town, and continues to be almost revered by the old timers of today. Woods Hall burned down in 1941.

The first Jumping Frog Jubilee and parade was held in Downtown Angels Camp in 1928. The celebration brought out a huge crowd.

Another photo of the '28 Jubilee. This shot was taken in front of the Commercial Hotel, with Woods Hall in the background.

The 1929 Jumping Frog Jubilee at the corner of Hardscrabble and Main Street. Note the "clothesline" with tin frogs and tree moss hanging on it. The Waverly Hotel is now Scott's Tavern, and the Star Saloon across the street is located in the Calaveras Hotel.

A brand new Basinett Hotel, Woods Hall far left, a 1930's photo.

Dollings Hall was another downtown dance hall. The uses of this hall were more varied. Not only operas and shows appeared there, but many celebrations were centered in Dollings Hall, which was built by Otto Dollings, then owner-operator of the Angels Hotel. This hall was located just behind, and a bit north of the hotel, and on a higher level than Main Street businesses. Cosgrove Hall, Tryon's Hall, and Dreamland Hall all played an important roll in varied celebrations. Another very popular dance hall was located just two hundred yards north of today's northern city boundary. This was Monte's Inn. The dancing there has long been discontinued, but the building is still there at the millennium, the only survivor of this group. At this writing, the hall looks like it wants to, or has already, given up. It is wooden, unpainted, and has the appearance of being in its last stage of life. It is located just 100 feet north of the Grub Stake Mini-Storage Units, on Highway 49, just north of the Angels Camp city limits.

Plays and operas were held in most of the halls from time to time. However, the first movie theatre in Angels Camp was the "Nickelodeon", a converted plumbing shop owned by the Love family. This theatre was located on the west side of downtown's Main Street, in the second block north of the bridge, just past the Calaveras Hotel.. It had a distinctive arched canope in front. The interior of the theater was a little crude, in that the seating consisted of simple, wooden benches. The floor was a dirt floor, covered with sawdust.

The ANGELS CAMP RACE TRACK was put together in 1894. Located in the area of what is now Frogtown RV facility, the track became an instant hit. It was organized by Charlie Tryon, Otto Dolling, John Meyers, Michael Arndt and Soloman King, and was incorporated under the name "The Angels Camp Race Track Association."

MIDWIFERY was widely practiced in the 19th century, and Angels Camp was no exception. Midwifery is the practice of assisting mothers-to-be with childbirth. Angels Camp had two ladies that practiced the art.

In the Purdyville area, Bonnie and Barney Baratono were raising chickens and selling eggs in 1934. Bonnie was a Registered Nurse, experienced in the art of birthing. They decided to open a midwifery, and called it the "Stork's Nest". Over the next eleven years she brought 210 babies into this world, two of which were twins. The Purdyville location of the "Stork's Nest" was on a street called *Stork Road.* Bonnie and Barney, the aunt and uncle of Police Chief George Baratono kept good records of their "new" clients. Another midwifery was operated by Adeline "Addie" Minard on Bush Street. She, too, assisted in about 200 births.

The *ANGELS GUN CLUB* just celebrated its 50th anniversary in the year 2000. It was "born" in Barney Bernasconi's Sierra Club banquet room in 1946. Those attending the confab were John Guttinger, Bill Collier, Mel Sorraco, Ken MacDonald, John Vierra, Bob Raggio, Joe Val, Jim Luly, Wint Whittle, Alvin Pecchenino, Norm Hickman, Harry Croshaw, Albert Pecchenino, and Elwood Hutchinson. Over the years the club has provided entertainment and recreation for literally hundreds of members and visitors. Dinner "meetings" are held each month on the first Friday, with a menu of steak, barbecued to perfection, mushroom stringbeans, mixed salad and sliced and buttered French bread. The club also holds an annual family day, and an annual crab feed. Shooting at the club usually occurs on Tuesday evenings, on a well-lighted trap range, equipped with three automatic electric traps (target throwers).

The construction of the clubhouse began in 1947. The labor was virtually 100 percent volunteer. It has since been enlarged more than three times its original size, and has been equipped with state-of-the-art equipment, including a barbecue that can cook over 200 steaks at one time. Today the club has five trap houses, a pistol range and a bench rest range for riflemen. The success of the organization can be attributed to the many members, officers and organizers. Here are just a few of the leaders who have made a difference: (in no specific order): Chris Porovich, Martin Errecart, Jim Valente, Milt Goodridge, George Porovich, Elmo Meyers, Kien McFall, Buck Segale, Guy Castle, Adolph and John Gualdoni, Ike Moore, James Tarbat, Doc Albasio, Dede Conrado, Harold Dillashaw, Howard Castle, Fritz Kneiff, Sid Kobleck, Corky Lombardi, Charlie Wells, Babe Stone, Albert Anderson, Bill Hoffman, Clyde Nash, Sam Marshall, Dave Verhalen, Guy Castle, and numerous others, the omission of which we apologize. The Angels Gun Club's success is shown in the look of members' faces on their way from the cook-house to the dining room each gathering.

The lady staff of the Calaveras Hotel, always immaculately dressed, poses for this 1890-91 photo. Top row, l to r, Susie Huberty, Millie Rolleri, 2nd row, Effie Johnston, Lizzie Huberty, Martha Johnston, Mary Huberty, Kate Zwinge, 3rd row, Josephine Bernasconi, Carrie Huberty and Lu Rolleri.

SOUTH OF THE CITY: By looking at the map of the entire Angels Camp district (next page), one can see that mining did not stop at the city limits. Dozens of mines were in operation from Albany Flat to Carson Hill and Melones.. Many did not make their owners rich, but several – especially the Morgan Mine – made their owners millionaires. If you compare the 1940's photo (see page 111) with today's view of the Morgan stope, you can see the massive deep pit mining of this claim. Millions were taken out of this mine even up until the 1990's.

Carson Hill produced more gold than Angels Camp. There was an active community there, also. The Angels Camp branch of the Sierra Railroad stopped at the Carson Hill station. Among others, note the Oneto Brothers store, a beehive of activity in Carson Hill. It was from this store that the Oneto family ranch on Highway 49 and Red Hill Road was developed.

One of Carson Hill's primary trading posts, the Oneto Bros. Store

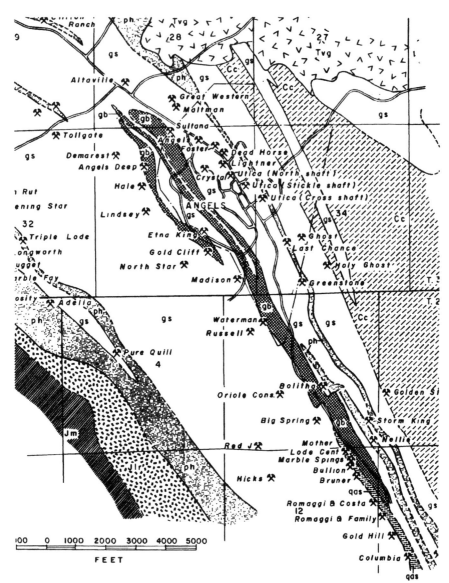

Courtesy of The State of California Division of Mines and Geology

Map of the Angels Camp District showing geology and lode mines.
Note the "string" of mines located on the Mother Lode main lode,
and the auxiliary lode which includes the Utica & Lightner Mines.

Courtesy of the State of California Division of Mines and Geology

Driving southbound on Highway 49, with Carson Hill in view, the Morgan stope is shown in this 1940's photo. Today, almost 60 years later, most of this mountain is gone, mined in the 1990's.

Ruth Lemue behind the front desk at the Angels Hotel.

MANY FORTUNES were made in Angels Camp. Some wealth moved on to become enormous fortunes, and some moved on to be lost. The residents of the Angels area have enjoyed such good fortune as an abundance of supurb mountain water, a healthy mix of agriculture, and a keen sense of neighborliness. The city is growing, and no doubt will continue to be a very pleasant place to live.

Chapter Ten –

A walking tour of Angels Camp

We'll start the tour at the Visitors Center, on Main Street at Rasberry Lane –Hardscrabble Street.Walk down the west side of the street, viewing the east side. The tour should take up to two hours if you walk the entire tour from Utica Park to just south of the Angels Creek bridge. Have fun, and watch your step.

1.   This is Rasberry Lane, named after one of the very earliest pioneers, & a successful miner during the Goldrush.

2.   The Veterams Memorial Building, built in 1966 of "classic Mother Lode architecture with arched windows, wooden balcony with turned-wood railing, exterior of slump stone." The building was built to house a new City Hall with veteran's facilities upstairs. The frontage on Main Street, in the old days prior to '66, had three buildings on it. On the corner was the Starcevich Saloon and miners clothing store. Next door a two-story building, downstairs was a tailor shop, upstairs was Hawley's law offices, followed by another tailor, Mr. A.H. Erickson, (also his home). Next, was John Davey's men's clothing. Later, a restaurant was here.

3.   In early days, this was the site of "Crooked Nose Joe's" (Porcella) Saloon and Bocci Alley. Dave Casseretti had his barber shop in a rear corner. Ben Curti later ran the Saloon. Then, "Freds Place" restaurant was run by Fred Jones. The store was also Miles Bettger's Furniture, afterward owned by C.A. Simondet. The entire store is now an artist's gallery.

4.   At one time a two-story building, housed Angels Camps Fire House consisting of one hose cart. The first chemical fire truck later housed here. A belltower atop the building signaled fires and curfews.This building was demolished and owner built the present building.

5.   Circus Hill stairs, leads up to a city parking lot. The stairs were the Main Street entrance to Stickle Theater and Dolling Hall located on the upper lot level, where it was said that Lola Montez and the Booths performed.

6.   This was a jewelry shop run by

7.   8.   9.   10.

Peter Johnson and later George Parker. It was also the site of Angel's Camp's first first Post Office , then a card room and tobacco store, a funeral home, then again a card room and tobacco shop, and is now the Pickle Barrel, a restaurant.

7.   Once a two-story building, housed the newspaper "Angels Camp Record", then the "Calaveras Californian". Jesse Mayo bought the business, and also ran a printing office. Another store was Wilson Insurance, earlier occupied by Ignatz Suess's tobacco shop, where he made his famous hand-made cigars. This was also the second location of the Post Office.

8.   The north half of this building was Mrs. Ervin's candy and ice cream shop, later sold to Mrs. Hugh Kennedy. Angels Food Market later occupied the space., its first location, then an optomitrist. The south half housed the Goodloe and Barden Drug Store. and soda foundain. This was also the third location of the Post Office. The present Turner's Western Wear store opened in 1977 in this space, then expanded to the entire double-store main floor.

9.   The Calaveras County Bank opened its doors here in 1900. Being a successful financial institution, the Bank of Italy in its expansion days bought the bank. A.P. Gianinni's empire then changed its name to the Bank of America. When the bank moved across the street, the store became the Calaveras Meat Market. Upstairs was occupied by the telephone exchange, which later became the offices of Drs. Wilson and Cooper, dentists.

10.   Stickle Building. The south (right) half of this building is one of the earliest buildings still standing, built in 1856 by the Stickle brothers, Ed and George, as a home for their general merchandise store. This is where the local housewife would buy fabrics, kitchenware and groceries. Later Patee Bros. and Taylor operated the store. The north half of the building was added several years after the original building. In the 1920's Turner Lillies Calaveras Transit purchased the building which became the main bus terminal in the county. Turner Lillie then also became Angels Camp's first Ford dealer, where he set up shop in the building. As the bus traffic waned, the building became Fenton Bolton's 5 & !0 Variety Store. When George Dietz purchased the Ford dealership, he occupied the entire building. The next businesses were Williams Auto Parts and

-114-

an automobile repair garage.

11.   This building was first a saloon, then Osborn's dry goods and variety. Carl Mills had a radio and repair shop while he was agent for the Stockton Record. Charles Crespi rebuilt the building, divided it into three stores. The Post Office, a men's store and an insurance office were occupants. Today, Tim Folendorf's The Land Company and a leather goods shop are tenants.

12.   This building, too, was first a saloon, then Charles Hyman's Mens Store. Epstein's Men's Store succeeded, then Frank Crespi operated the store., and his nephew, Bob Gianelli continued on with Bob's Mens' Clothing for many years. The present tenant is Lost Hills' mens and ladies clothing and accessories.

13.   The A. Brosemer Building, built in 1889, had law offices and a men's store then Dr. Lamb, Dr. Noetling, and Dr. Albasio had their offices, and now law offices, all upstairs. Downstairs started with Mike Arndt's store for men, then a meat market, barber shop, Phillip's Dry Goods Store, and today a Coin Shop.

14.   This mercantile store started as Mose Arndt's dry goods. Circa 1900 a new building housed Philip Pache's dry goods. Next, Mitchell Pusich's grocery store occupied this larger property, until Bolton's variety store moved in in the 1930's. Tony Zanardi's hardware then opened here until the Mercantile Store became the current occupant.

15.   I.O.O.F. Building – the lodge and offices are upstairs, and continue to have regular Odd Fellows meetings. Downstairs was Jake Ayala's Saloon, followed by Phillips dry goods and Peachy's Cigar Store, each with half. Mr. R. Rasmussen succeeded in the dry goods store. Then, George Kenny moved the Railway Express office into the building. Frank Stephens and Ray Kern were later agents, then agent Ray O'Connor shared the office with Earle Edminston, who operated a photo studio.

16.   The Dolling Building was built by Otto Dolling after he became the owner-operator of the Angels Hotel in 1888. The upstairs became additional rooms for the hotel, and the downstairs was occupied by Davey and Carley's Store, then in 1900 became a bar that was part of the hotel. The bar then became the hotel's dining room, until in 1945 Mrs. Rolleri Grillo bought the building for a dry goods store. Don Spreadborough then purchased it, converted the upstairs into apartments, and the lower floor became a

17.   18.   19.   20.   21.

bakery. It is now vacant in transition.

17.   Angels Hotel is the crown jewel of Angels Camp's historic buildings. Although no longer a hotel, this building served as the core center of the city's social activity, plus being the location where Mark Twain found "Simon Wheeler dozing comfortably by the bar-room stove"... and his story of Jim Smiley's obsession to bet on anything, especially a contest between two frogs. And this hotel had a wide reputation of extraordinary service, food and drink. All of its owners continued the reputation until it was finally turned into an apartment house (upstairs) by Gerald Heintz, as it remains today. The street level now houses an auto & boat accessories store, and an attorney's office.

18.   Birds Way. This street was originally the eastbound exit from downtown, toward Vallecito and Murphys. About 90 years ago, the county and state built the (2) bridges, widened and paved the highway, and moved the eastbound exit a ½ block to the south, then made Birds Way a blind street.

        Birds Way was the Chinatown of Angels Camp, which had an extensive Chinese population of up to 4,000. They had their own cemetery, and grew vege-

tables on the hillside. This was also a location for the ladies of the evening. The city jail was situated just 200 feet down the left side. It is still in existence, and is a law office now. It is worth the walk to go down and view it. Two other buildings are worthy of mention here. The Pierano Store, Angels Camps' first "fire-proof" mercantile store built in 1855 (see picture on page 3), with frontage on Main Street, at Birds Way — the southeast corner. The other notable building is Joseph Pierano's home, also built of stone, behind the store. on Birds Way. It is still standing, and has been occupied continuously since the 1850's by Joseph Pierano's heirs.

19.   The Vintage Realty-Fidelity Savings Building is relatively new. It is located on the exact same site as the Pierano Store.

20.   Office Building, this, too, is a relatively new structure. Built just recently, this building is the first building to be built here. It served as Carley's used car lot earlier.

21.   Angels Creek. This creek was a simple mountain creek, drying up each year in the mid-summer. In the latter pert of the 1800's the creek became an important part of the restructuring of the river and creek water flow in the county.

-116-

22.   23.   24.

The portion of the creek flowing under these bridges is filled with three important water-rights sources: first, the upstream property owners are guaranteed a constant (minimal) flow; second, the water used to power the electricity-generating plant just 300 yards upstream, empties into the creek; and third, the run-off from the local hills, plus the overflow of the city water system.

Angels Creek went on a rampage in 1909, overflowed its banks, and caused very extensive damage to creekside buildings and bridges. It is now well-stocked with native trout by State Fish and Game.

The bridges were rebuilt in 1909 by the county and state..

THREE SITES JUST SOUTH OF THE BRIDGE

22.   The was the site of Joseph Pierano's first home. When Caltrans widened the highway, his home was demolished and the creek was realigned over much of his property.

23.   Dr. George Pashe's home was built in the 1880's by the Utica Mining Company as an incentive for him to participate in the mines medical needs.

He was a very critical part of the early years local medicine. With no hospitals, the doctors had to improvise with their offices and clinics, and have a bed or two available for medical use. The home was rebuilt in 1994-96, and is now commercial and professional offices.

24.   The FOURTH home on the left was the Utica Hospital. In 1894 the mines were plagued with numerous accidents which prompted the miners to rebel. The Utica Mining Company was "forced" to build a hospital to care for these injuries. It built the facility, which housed eight patients on the second floor ward, and eight more on the first floor ward. Dr. George Pasche was in charge of the hospital.

The building was sold and converted into apartments. It has served many families since the mines closed in the 1915-20 period. No other hospital replaced this hospital. Mark Twain-St. Josephs Hospital in San Andreas remains the only hospital in Calaveras County.

25.   The site between Angels Creek and Finnegan Lane was the site of Angels Camp's first structure. Henry and George Angel established their Trading Post here. Scribner and Matthews took over the following year and continued in this

location until burned out, and moved into the Wells Fargo Building (#29). The next structure in this location was a plain old building, but of major importance. This two-story wooden structure was built in 1890 by Joseph Pierano as a rooming house, and faced Main Street, with its long side running down Finnegan Lane. . In 1900 a French Hand Laundry and a plumbing shop occupied the main floor. In 1909 the creek flooded and caused major damage. The building was elevated several feet, a porch was added, and in 1918 a mortuary moved in. The rooming house ceased to exist, and in 1945, a portion of the first floor became a meeting hall for two churches. Then, in 1949, the City Hall took occupancy after moving out of its temporary home in the Angels Hotel (City Hall had been burned out of the Woods Building, its original location). City Hall continued occupancy until its "new" quarters in the Veterans Building was completed in 1966.

The city's Police Chief, George Baratono, and the Judicial Court made this their home until the building was demolished soon thereafter. A new building at this location has housed a "4x4 ATV" shop, and now serves as a wood carving shop.

26.   Finnegan Lane. This street was one of the earliest residential neighborhoods in the city, along with Bush Street. It is still one of the prominent locations of some of the older, early homes.

27.   Carley's Garage. This location was originally a blacksmith shop, and was washed away in the flood of 1909. Rebuilt immediately, the Carley family successfully operated a garage and auto agency here for many years.

The present occupant is the Thrift Shop of Mark Twain-St. Joseph's Hospital.

28.   This parking lot was the site of one of the city's favorite dance halls, Woods Hall. The building was called the Wells Fargo Building, and had a very colorful history of tenants. After being built as a one-story building, the demand for space became so heavy that a second story was added, and a new face was put on the entire building. The hall was on the second story.

Scribner and Mathews moved their trading post from its original creek-side location into the Wells Fargo Building. Dr. Dorrah had his office here, and Rasmussen's Grocery along with Wells Fargo Express were located here.

Angels Camp's first City Hall also became a part of this building. A doctor, a dentist and a lawyer practiced here, as did a barber shop — last occupied by Walter Valente. Woods Hall was more than just a popular dance hall. It was on the Chattaqua Circuit for vaudeville acts. Many entertainers of their day were billed here. Subsequent tenants were a dress shop, drug store, and an ice cream shop. Fire destroyed the complex in 1931.

29.   Bazinett Hotel. Many businesses occupied this property prior to the present-day hotel. Frank Washburn's and Louis Raggio's Louvre Saloon, R. Rasmussen's tailor shop, and Mrs. Eddy's Commercial Hotel. Charles Powell ran the hotel later. Then Jim Jack had his general store, which became Tim Adam's tin shop, which was succeeded by Ed Siegel's Sporting Goods Store.

All of these businesses were destroyed by the 1931 fire that originated in a rear storage room of the Commercial Hotel. The Utica House Hotel (nee Bazinett Hotel), a fire-resistant structure was erected almost immediately. The Bazinett Building's storefront tenants were, from the south, Safeway succeeded by Angels Food Market succeeded by today's Orphan Annies Emporium (a co-op of 40 antique dealers), then a beauty shop now a picture frame shop, the hotel lobby, with the hotel's coffee shop on the north. A popular saloon was located in the basement area, under the hotel's main lobby, with a street entrance, now closed.

31.   32.   33.   34. 35. 36.

30.   Today's occupant is Diana's Dolls and Things. The previous store was Floozy's Dress Shop. (actually the most northerly storefront in the Bazinett).
31.   BofA Cafe. This location originally had several businesses on it. Fred Ratz's Barber Shop, later owned by Al Graebe, then Nels Moller, then Harry Garett's Saloon, then Sylvia Murray's gift shop all resided here. All of these buildings all were destroyed in the fire of 1931.

      The Bank of America built a new building, and occupied this location for many years, until the bank built bigger quarters uptown, across from Save Mart Supermarket in Altaville. When they moved out, the property was remodeled into several inside shops. When the "BofA Café'" opened, they further remodeled and are thriving today.
32.   In the 1890's the City Drug Store, operated by Dr. Dorrah, also housed the city's first telephone exchange. This location has also been the home of Angels Appliance Store, George Parker's jewelry store , O.J.Scherer Company, and Angels Camp's first Safeway Store. It is now in transition. (empty).
33.   Early-day saloons occupied this building. There was Mayer's Saloon, then

Bert Morgan's The Davey Crockett Saloon, which boasted that Mark Twain rode his horse inside, tied it up, and turned around and ordered at the bar. Robert Lillie's Saloon followed, and was the home of the Angels Baseball Club. Charlie Crespi started his Men's Store here, then moved across the street. Marie's Dress Shop then occupied the store for many years, and is now Nellie Lou's Antiques.
34.   Built in the 1890's as Rose's Butcher Shop, then became Fred Heller's Butcher Shop. Today's occupant is Country Manor Interiors.
35.   The left half of this building is occupied by a local newspaper, The Ledger Dispatch. Its original occupant was the Hyman Bros. "Red Front Store", then came the post office, then the telephone exchange (third location). The right half is the home of Sue's Angels Creek Café and her giant pancakes and delicious sandwiches.
36.   Alley to the back city parking lot. A very popular Chinese café was situated in the back corner of this parking lot. It was demolished long ago.
37.   This building was originally built in the 1860's as a warehouse for the Stickle Store located across the street. Then Joe Raggio ran a saloon, succeeded

-120-

by Rollie Raggio's saloon and pool hall. Earl Chapman bought the business, which was purchased by Vincent Raggio. This was followed by the Sierra Club Café, operated by the Oliver "Barney" Bernasconi family. They served delicious Chinese and American food for years. Next door, first came Dan Holmes' saloon, followed by Si and Nick's, then Ernest Soracco's saloon. The Bernasconis bought the saloon and ran in along with their café. They closed their door and Cruscos Italian Restaurant became today's occupant.

38.   For years this site was a Saloon and card room. It then became the Pioneer Club, a bar and card room run by the Bernasconi family. Today, this location is The Taylor Collection, an art gallery.

39.   The Angels Theater Building – The storefront occupant on the left is and insurance office owned by Fire Chief Roy Soracco and Terry Bullock. Then the theater entrance (three screens), then a nail/beauty schop.

40.   The present Angels Camp Post Office now occupies this property, but an early-day store housed an ice cream parlor on one side, and Mr. Mosgrove's then Bill Loves jewelry shop. Later Charlie Miller built a stone building which housed

both a grocery store and a tailor shop, and then Fishbeck's Furniture store. The post office moved into this property in the 1960, and has occupied ever since.

41.   This small shop has been a crafts and curio shop,now vacant.

42.   Scott's Tavern - This is the last saloon to survive in Angels Camp. At one time over 40 saloons were in operation. Just prior to Scott's Tavern, "Mels Corner" was here more than three decades. This property started out as Frank Egan's Central Park Hotel. Next it was Edie Rakovich's Waverly Hotel, and also served as a stage stop in Angels Camp.

43.   Hardscrabble Lane with its "Chicken Ladder" sidewalk (one-way steep street). See frontispiece photo.

44.   Visitors Center and parking facility. This corner and entire block was a very busy part of downtown in earlier times. Ralph Lemue's blacksmith shop was the first business on this corner. In the late 1800's it was demolished and a new two-story building erected. Walter Pettit's Star Saloon was situated on the corner (see photo on p. 105), with diagonal corner doors. The second story was all part of Olivia Rolleri's Calaveras Hotel . Today, of course, the new Visitors Center, Visitors Bureau and parking and restroom

facilities, jointly sponsored by the city and Caltrans.

45.   The next two hundred feet or so was the fabulous Calaveras Hotel. This was operated by the very capable Olivia Rolleri (see p. 82). Raggio's Meat Market was a frontage tenant, as were other businesses from time to time.

46.   Angels Movie Theater, originally a small tin shop and plumbing shop, was the first movie house in Angels Camp. It was a crude little theater, with benches and sawdust in lieu of loges and carpet.

47.   The first businesses here were A. Love's dairy and livery stable. They flourished for years, when Mr. Love covered the ground with a cement slab, and converted the stable into an auto garage. It was finally demolished, but the slab still remains as a reminder of years of work with horses, buggies, and buckboards.

48.   The next property is a lawn, out in front of the Love's home, built c. 1855. The house also fronts on Bush Street, and is presently an antique store. The Vegia Saloon fronted on Main Street in the early days.

49.   This home is the Lagomarsino family home. Mr. Lagomarsino was the

owner of the early-day Lagomarsino and Bacigalupi Grocery store across the street.

50.   Thomas Repair Shop, also was a tin shop, Mr. Siegel had a blacksmith shop here, later became Joe Zwinge's auto repair shop, who was bought out by Mr. Miladinovich. Then, two small homes.

51.   Pine Street

52.   This next block is now almost entirely an auto show lot. In early days, the home of John and Louisa Rice, the Magud home, and a boarding house with a small saloon were in this block.

Portions of this block were stacked high with logs and lumber for use in the Utica mines.

An auto accessories and parts store now occupies the north corner lot.

53.   Sam's Way

54.   This was the home of the North and South Shafts of the Utica Mine. (The south shaft was technically located across the highway). The hoisting works, stamp mill, and other infrastructures of the mine were located here. Take note of the two skips still forming an entranceway to the park on Sam's Way. These were actual skips used to hoist and lower the miners and ores up and down the mine shafts. The entire block is now the city owned Utica Park. The gazebo was transported

61,   62,   63,   64.

from the Brewery just south of the bridge. Take note that this entire park is located in a sink, where the mine caved in and lowered the surface of the ground.

The mansion located just west of the park is the Utica Mansion, or Lane Mansion, originally built by the owner of the Utica Mine, and then served as the home of the mine's superintendent for many years. It is presently the private residence of the Tad Folendorf family.

55.   On the northern boundary of Utica Park lies the hoisting machinery that was used by the next-door Lightner Mine. It is interesting if you're a machinery buff, but be careful crawling around it. It's a little hazardous. Today, it is a bit covered by some bushes and trees.

56.   Across Main Street, Hwy. 49, lies a gas station. This was originally the space for the site of the South Shaft of the Utica Mine.

57.   Bret Harte Rd. (south)

58.   The county's prime mortuary is situated on this corner.

59.   Just south, the Auto dealership of the Wilmshurst family. The Stickle mine shaft was just uphill a few feet.

60.   The First Congregational Church, dedicated in 1905, was to the rear and above the present church.

61.   Church Street

62.   This home was the residence of the John Pierano family. It then became the Monte Verda home, and has just recently changed hands.

63.   The Pierano Building, was built for his grocery store and bar. The business was sold to Lagomarsino and Bacigalupi. It is presently occupied by the GoldRush World Access, an internet provider.

64.   This was the location for the Carpenters Union Hall. It then became The Calaveras Printing Shop, operated for two generations by the Luly family.

65.   The site for many various stores. It was a branch library recently.

66.   The Lode Hotel Building is located on the site of Benegar Rasberry's original – and very rich – gold claim which stretches to the corner. The present two-story building was built by the James Girardi family in 1890, as a rooming house, saloon and Italian restaurant. The second floor has evolved into apartments, now owned by the Moore family.

67.   This 2-story rooming house has housed a miner's liquor store, barber shop, insurance office, and is now home of a Beauty Shop and the Angels Jewelers.

THIS CONCLUDES the walking tour. We hope you've enjoyed it.

65,   66,   67.

Bibliography

Pioneer Days of Angel's Camp, Edna Bryan Buckbee, 1932

A Brief History of Angels Camp, Edward C. Leonard, 1998

Historic Spots in California, Hoover, Rensch & Rensch,
      Stanford University Press, 1966

Las Calaveras, A Quarterly Bulletin of the Calaveras County
      Historical Society, numerous issues.

The Mother Lode Country, A Geologic Guidebook, Bulletin 141,
      State of California, Division of Mines and Geology, 1948

Calaveras County, California, County Report Number Two,
      State of California, Division of Mines and Geology, 1962

Gold Districts of California, Bulletin 193, State of California,
      Division of Mines and Geology, 1970

      Sierra Railway, Dorothy Newell Deane, Howell-North
      Publishers, Berkeley, California, 1960

Churches of Angels Camp, a report by Edward C. Leonard and
      Bessie McGinnis, 1982, courtesy of Calaveras Historical
      Society

An Album of the Pioneer Schools of Calaveras County, compiled
      and published by the Calaveras County Historical Society.

Bret Harte, a Biography, Richard O'Connor, Little, Brown & Co.,
      Boston, 1966

The Sagebrush Bohemian, Mark Twain in California, Nigey
      Lemon, Paragon House, New York, 1990

San Joaquin Historian, a quarterly journal of the San Joaquin
      County Historical Society, Vol. 13, No. 1, Spring 1999,
      titled *Turner Lillie's Calaveras Transit 1914 to 1941*,
      an article authored by C. R. Haynes.